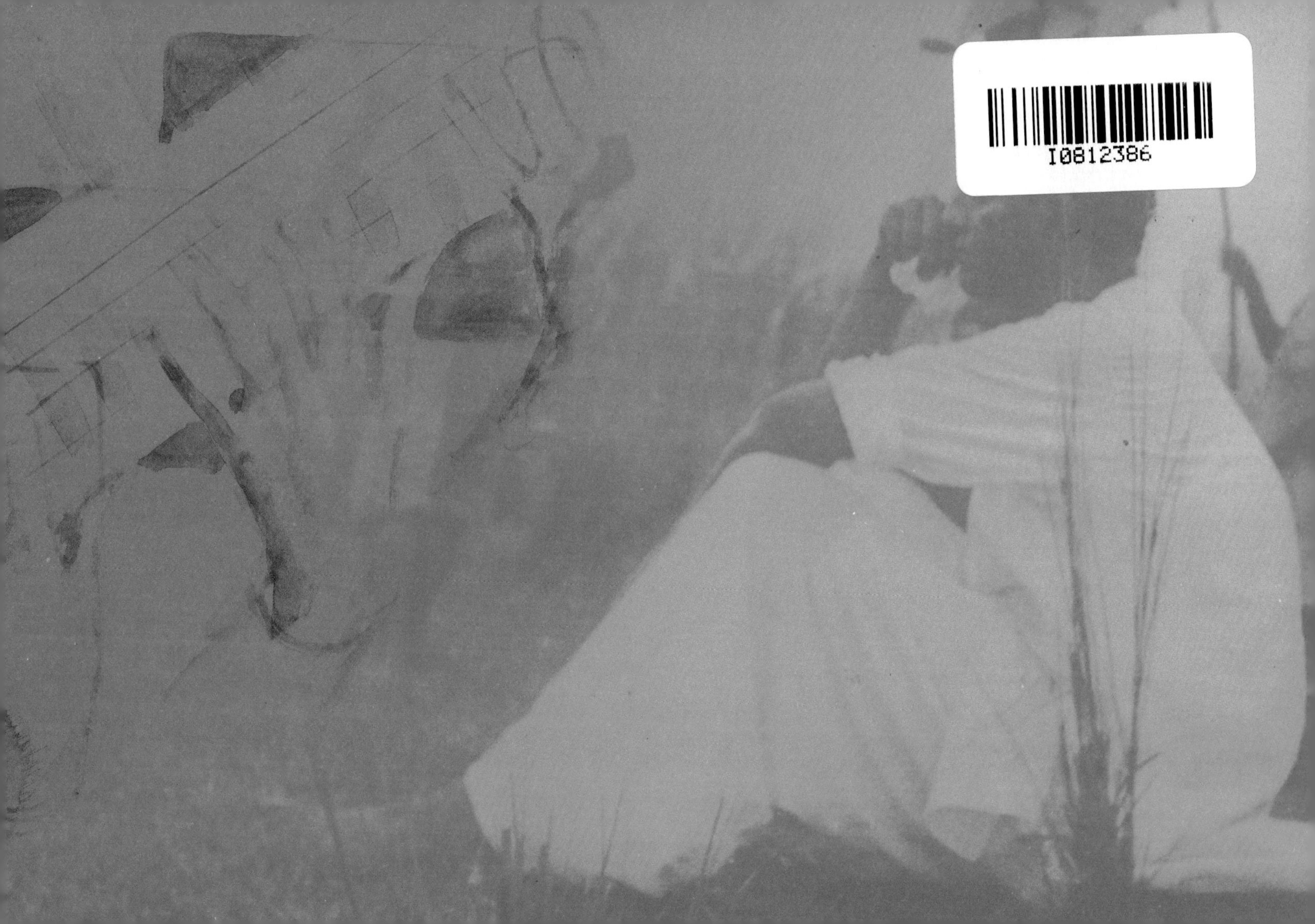

Satyajit Ray's Ravi Shankar

An Unfilmed Visual Script

A SITAR RECITAL

BY

Ravishankar

Satyajit Ray's Ravi Shankar

An Unfilmed Visual Script

Edited by Sandip Ray
in association with
Dhritiman Chaterji, Arup K. De, Deepak Mukerjee, Debasis Mukhopadhyay

Introduction by Sankarlal Bhattacharjee

Collins

Society for the Preservation of Satyajit Ray Archives

First published in India in 2014 by Collins
An imprint of HarperCollins *Publishers* India
In association with the Society for the Preservation of Satyajit Ray Archives

ISBN: 978-93-5136-174-9

2 4 6 8 10 9 7 5 3 1

HarperCollins *Publishers*
A-53, Sector 57, Noida, Uttar Pradesh 201301, India
77-85 Fulham Palace Road, London W6 8JB, United Kingdom
Hazelton Lanes, 55 Avenue Road, Suite 2900, Toronto, Ontario M5R 3L2
and 1995 Markham Road, Scarborough, Ontario M1B 5M8, Canada
25 Ryde Road, Pymble, Sydney, NSW 2073, Australia
31 View Road, Glenfield, Auckland 10, New Zealand
10 East 53rd Street, New York NY 10022, USA

Designed by Arijit Ganguly

Printed and bound at
Thomson Press (India) Ltd.

CONTENTS

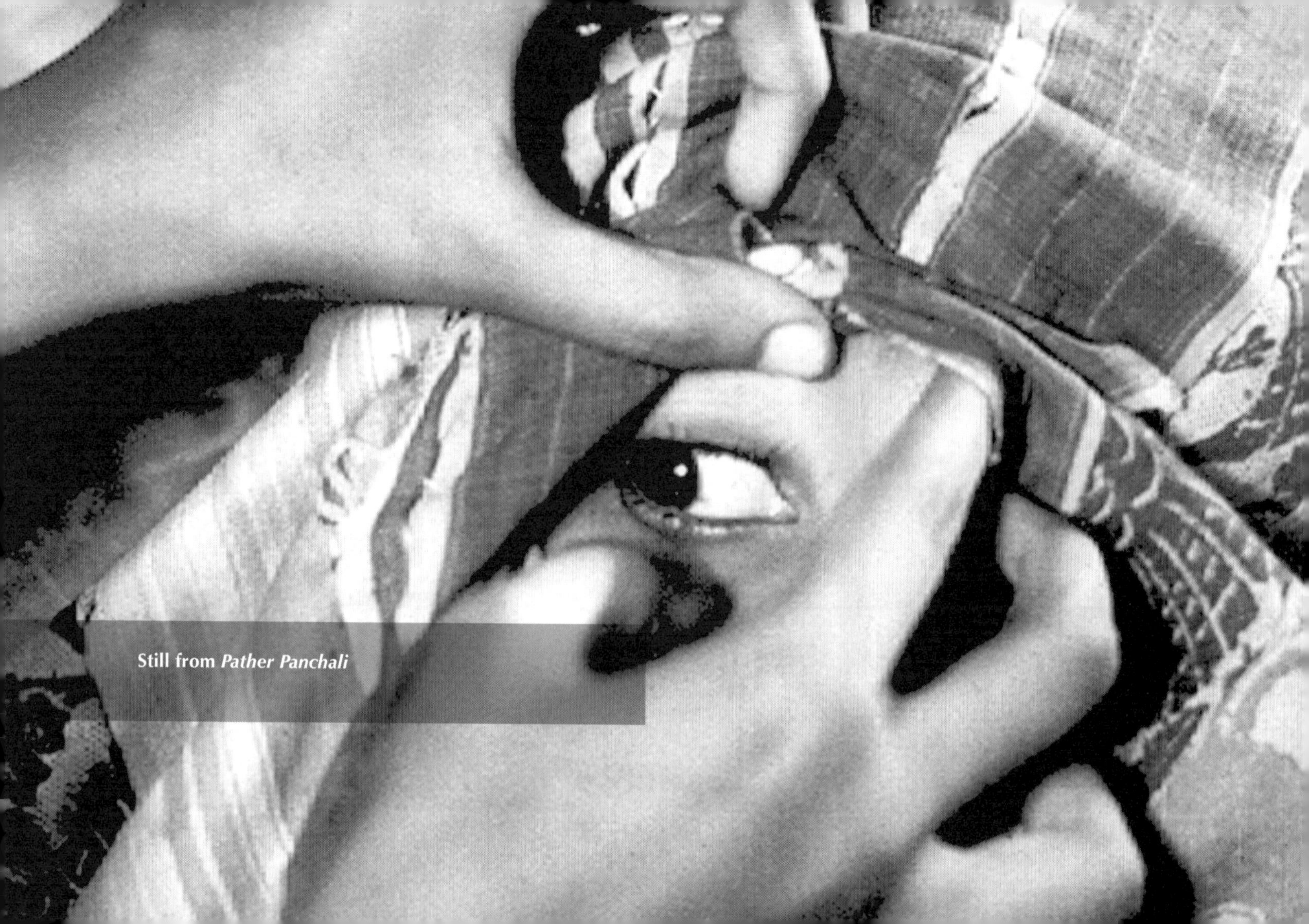

Still from *Pather Panchali*

PREFACE

I was born in a house in Lake Avenue, Kolkata, in 1953, and lived there till 1959. Ravi Shankar-ji came there quite a few times to see my father, Satyajit Ray. But I do not have any recollection of those meetings. It was in 1959 that Ravi-ji and Baba worked together for the last time on a film (*Apur Sansar*). Then we moved to another house in Lake Temple Road and thence to yet another in Bishop Lefroy Road where Baba lived from 1970 till 1992. Ravi-ji was already a busy musician when Baba requested him to compose the background score for *Pather Panchali*, his debut film. After that he did the music for *Aparajito*, *Paras Pathar* and *Apur Sansar*. They never worked together thereafter because Baba began to compose music for his own films in 1961. But their relations remained as close and congenial as before. Their friendship was based on mutual admiration which lasted till Baba breathed his last. How deeply Ravi-ji was affected by Baba's passing could be gauged by the fact that he immediately paid him a soulful tribute through his *Farewell, My Friend*. The album was released at the Grand Hotel in Kolkata and we attended the launch.

Ravi-ji was a quintessential Bengali bhadralok though he led a cosmopolitan life most of the time.

He lived abroad for long periods of time and became a globetrotter. But, strangely enough, he never gave up his Bengali lifestyle. His love for the Bengali language, culture and food was proverbial. Whenever he came to Kolkata for recitals, he tried to manage time to see Baba despite his tight schedules. 'Cholun mashai, ektu adda mara jaak (Let's meet and have a chat),' he would say. And they talked about nearly everything under the sun, in chaste Bengali, during those adda sessions.

Ravi-ji's worldwide fame as a sitar maestro obscured his vocal talents. He presented Baba with an LP record where he explained various Indian ragas and raginis. It was meant primarily for a foreign audience. He sang a Holi song there which impressed Baba very much. Incidentally, many classical musicians were good vocalists as well. Ustad Vilayat Khan Sahib was one of them. He sang the song to which Roshan Kumari gave her dance performance in *Jalsaghar*.

We went to Benares to shoot for *Jai Baba Felunath* in the winter of 1977. Ravi-ji was then in Benares too. As soon as he came to know about us, he invited Baba to his place and insisted he come along with all his actors and unit people. Ravi-ji's nephew Ananda Shankar and his wife Tanushree were then staying with him. We went there along with Soumitra Chatterjee and Santosh Datta. We spent a whole day in the company of Ravi-ji. He showed us round a large plot of land adjacent to his house saying that he had decided to set up his music academy on that spot. 'It has always been my ambition to have my own teaching institution in India,' he said.

Those who know well about my father's work know that Baba made a storyboard for a short film on Ravi-ji in the early phase of his career as a film-maker, though it is not yet conclusively known exactly when he did so. Nor is it known why it did not turn into a film. According to Marie Seton, Baba's biographer, the storyboard was made in 1951. But there are film scholars who argue against this date. Whatever the date may have been, it may not be unreasonable to say that the storyboard was made before the time of *Aparajito*. For Baba left drawing blocks and used red notebooks (kheror khata) for the first time to write the screenplay for his second feature film.

The storyboard on Ravi Shankar-ji was a visual one, full of sketches drawn in the very manner of that for *Pather Panchali*. The 32-page drawing book, containing over a hundred sketches and some technical instructions on camera movements and other things, has been carefully preserved in the archives of our Society for a long time.

We decided to send it to print in the hope that a facsimile edition would give the admirers of my father the world over an idea of the format he chose for making his very early films. This is the first time a whole storyboard comprising sketches by my father is going to appear in book form. We are sure it will be a treat for readers.

We owe our thanks to D.N. Ghosh, the president of our Society and a distinguished author himself, and all our members for the unstinted encouragement we have received from them in bringing out this book. We would also like to say 'Thank You' to V.K. Karthika and Shantanu Ray Chaudhuri, publisher and managing editor, respectively, of HarperCollins for collaborating with our Society on a second Ray publication, the first having been *Deep Focus: Reflections on Cinema* that came out in December 2011.

Sandip Ray
Member-Secretary
Society for the Preservation of
Satyajit Ray Archives
(Formerly Society for the Preservation of
Satyajit Ray Films)
Kolkata

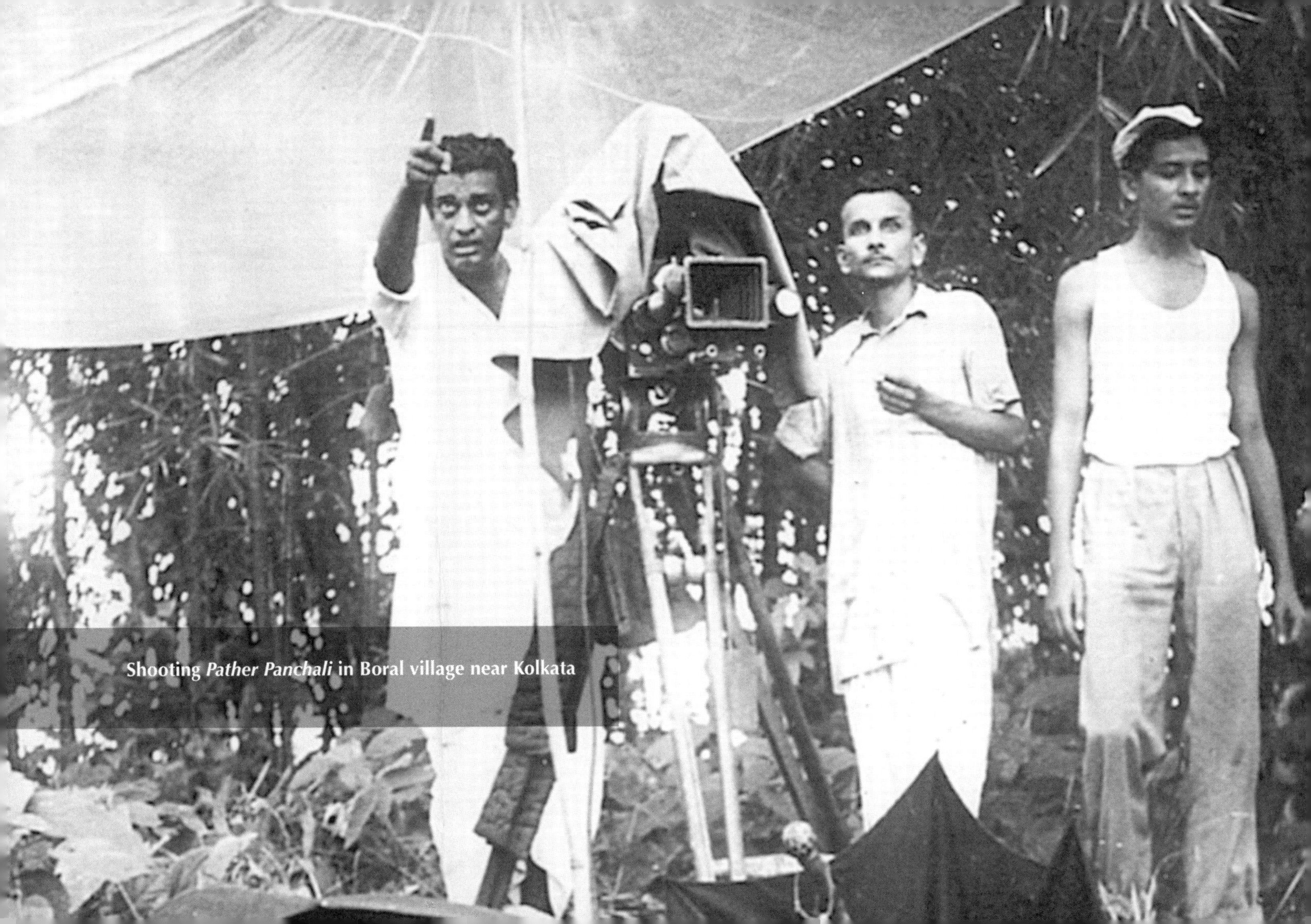

Shooting *Pather Panchali* in Boral village near Kolkata

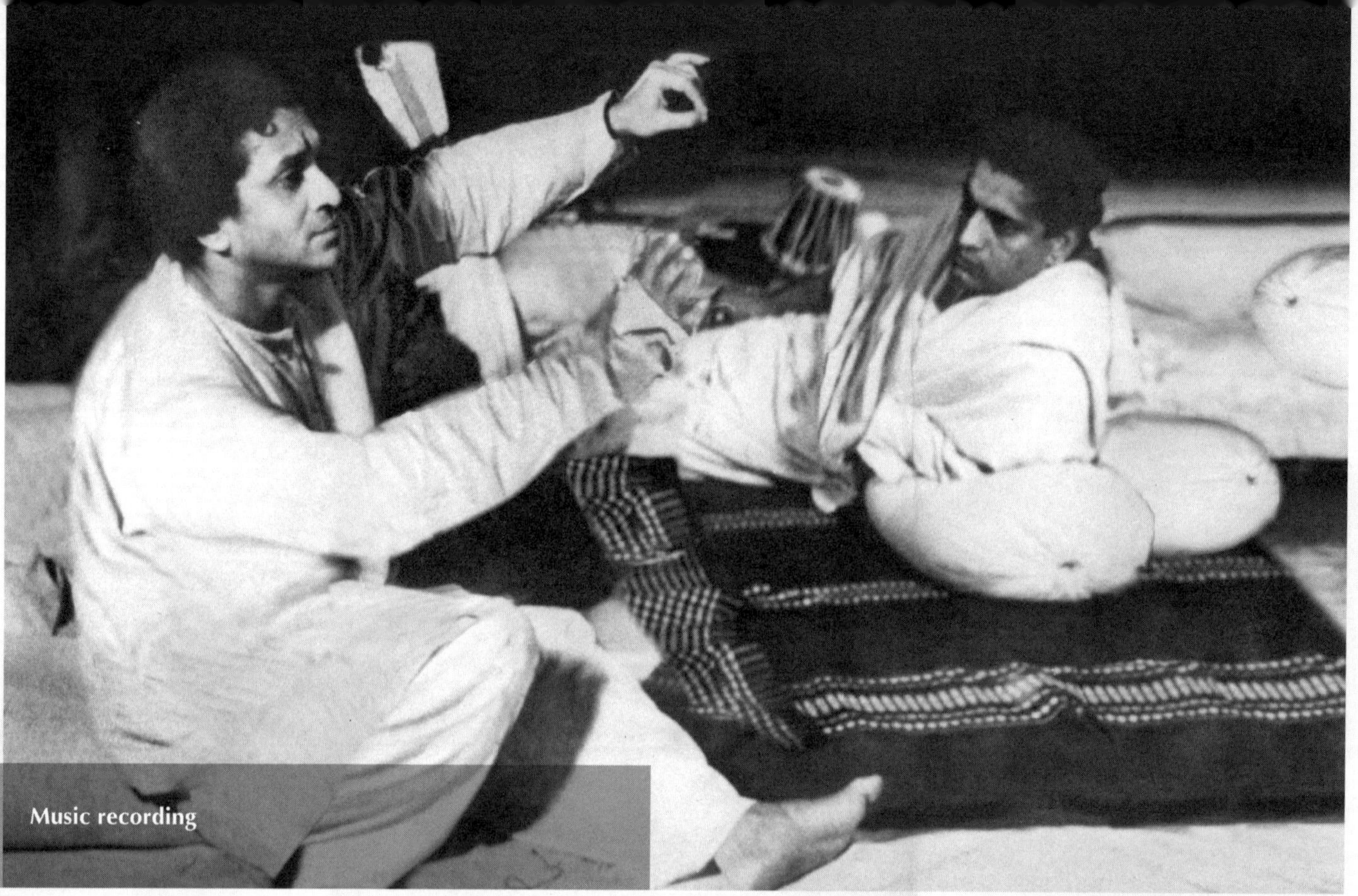

Music recording

UNHEARD MELODIES

THE SITAR AND THE CAMERA

Sankarlal Bhattacharjee

This is the story of a film that did not happen. This is a sitar recital by Ravi Shankar no one chanced to hear. This is one of two unrequited love affairs of Satyajit Ray with the motion picture. A documentary based on a concert, this is an attempt to combine the pleasures of the ear with those of the eye. Like the other film, a fantasy feature titled *The Alien*, that lies buried in an extraordinarily written screenplay, this too, titled *A Sitar Recital by Ravi Shankar*, is a script that encompasses a concert from alap to jhala, movement to movement, held only in pictures.

Ray's essay 'Ordeals of the Alien' details why *The Alien* could never be made, but he left no record of why the film on the concert suffered a similar fate. In response to my question on this in 1977, Ravi Shankar said:

'You asked about his film on me. Yes, he did have a plan of the kind. Amazingly, he had sketched the whole album on how the movie would go ... It was probably before he made *Aparajito* and I was then putting up at Jnanprakash Ghosh's in Calcutta. What I saw in there was: I am playing. The film draws ideas from the melodies and soars into images of trees, storms and springs ... gradually dissolving the sounds into the images. Then something happened, what really I cannot pinpoint, and the project lay suspended. There has been no further contact on this since.'

In her book *Satyajit Ray: Portrait of a Director*, Marie Seton, however, puts 1951 as the year of the sketches of the documentary. If that is so, they precede the making of *Pather Panchali*, which again, seems unlikely. In her book, published in 1977, Seton had hoped that the musical short could still be made.

In early 1978, when Ravi Shankar's photo-biographer Aloke Mitra went to Ray with his trove of images and requested a cover design, the latter readily agreed and patiently went through the album, stopping now and then to admire a shot or mood. After a long look at a portrait of Ravi Shankar against the backdrop of the Ganga at Benares, Ray had reportedly commented with a sigh, 'Oh-ho, he's gotten old!' When Aloke related this incident to me, I could immediately identify the cause of Ray's anxiety: he could see no future for the script on Ravi Shankar.

Exhuming the Ravi Shankar script after all these years does not reveal much regarding the visuals because we lack Ray's own narrative on the scheme. To begin with, we do not know what raga he intended Ravi Shankar to perform. The two hints that we can possibly derive from the album posit a quandary—the frame suggesting an evening landscape proposes a different time of day from the ones portraying a Rajasthani miniature built around the morning Ragini Todi. Also included is the sequence of a storm. With no raga identified, we are hard-pressed to gauge whether the image travels with the melodic content or simply reflects the speed generated on the strings. The reasoning behind finally settling on Raga Desh is part of the story I wish to narrate in this essay.

In the essay 'Some Aspects of My Craft', in 1966,

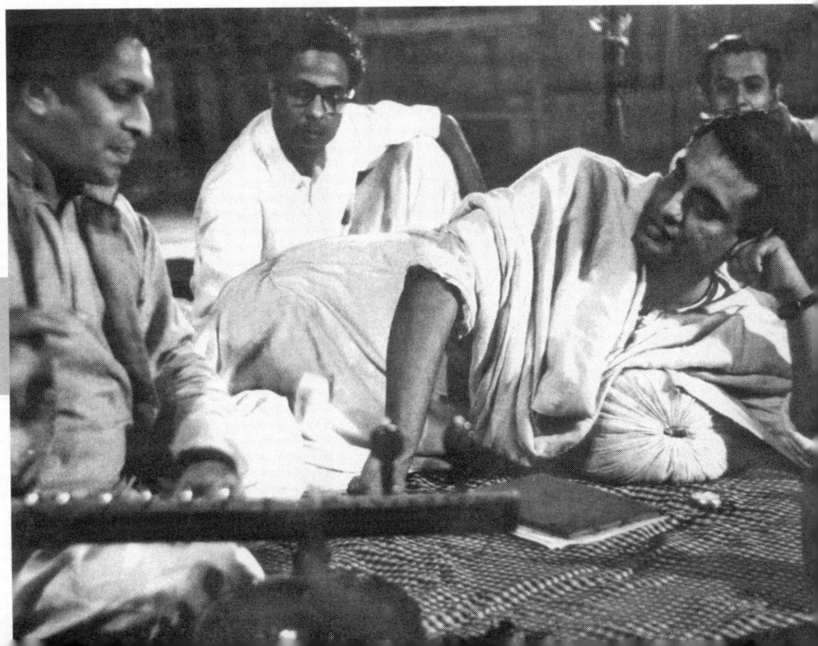

Music recording

Ray had stated his reasons for no longer working with professional composers. His argument was:

'Since *Teen Kanya* I have taken to composing the music for my own films. Before that I had worked with Ravi Shankar (four times), Ali Akbar Khan and Vilayat Khan (once each). The reason why I do not work with professional composers any more is that I get too many ideas of my own, and composers, understandably enough, resent being guided too much.'

If resentment over being guided too much is what caused Ravi Shankar to drift away from Ray, then the process commenced at about the same time as the music composition for *Aparajito* and the sketches for *A Sitar Recital by Ravi Shankar*. In his Bengali memoirs, *Smriti*, Ravi Shankar draws an exquisite word picture of the initial days of their collaboration and then drops a hint regarding the ensuing rift:

'To me our very own Satyajit Ray is a special creator compared to all of these I mention (great film-makers of the world). I was so very involved with him from the very beginning that a certain sentiment comes into play. I had been with him in his first film, then his second, third and fourth film. In a way we sort of grew up together. So I tend to get sentimental and personal when considering his work. I have a deep feeling and a special weakness for him, and, consequently, cannot have an impersonal judgement on anything about him. I cannot forget the impression left by his first work, *Pather Panchali*.

'It was, I remember, 1951 or '52. I was at Jnan-da's (Jnanprakash Ghosh), when he came to see me about this film. I, of course, had known him much prior to that and even heard from different sources that he was extremely eager to make a good film. So when he came and narrated the ordeals he had undergone to put together his movie ... how Dr B.C. Roy had come to his rescue ... I was overly impressed by his dedication. I could see that the gentleman was wading through one crisis after another. At the time of our meeting he was veritably surrounded by pressures. He then made the offer: "It would be nice if you would compose for the film. That will lend prestige to it too."

'Frankly, I had quite some fame then in India, though not abroad. I was known everywhere in the country, be it the music world or the art circles. So after the conversation, he arranged for a show at Bhavani cinema. Rushes. But I was spellbound by the rushes. Rush prints, you know, are the coarse stages of a film. Since I had been involved with the film medium from my younger days, I could extract a sense of things even from rushes. And viewing the rushes of *Pather Panchali* I instantly knew I was in the presence of a masterpiece. It was so replete with realism, yet plucked at all the chords of your heart. Besides I had read *Pather Panchali* and *Aparajito* when I was very young as they were serialized in *Bharatbarsha* ...The novels had stayed on with me as a personal experience since then. I saw that gentle and beautiful *Pather Panchali* revealing itself in pictures in Satyajit-babu's work. I was moved and felt immensely inspired. I said, "What are you saying? How can I not do music for this film?"

'Satyajit-babu was obviously a bit low in spirits though there was no dearth of self-confidence. He knew at heart that he had made something solid, but was concerned about how the audience would react to such a realistic film. Yet it was that realism that had drawn me to it, and I told him I would gladly compose for the film and deem it an honour. And then everything happened in a rush.

'I saw the film once again. Then a studio was booked for a day. All I can remember is that the scoring was over in four or five hours. We had about six or seven hands. The music too reaped a world of praise alongside the movie because of its spontaneous outflow. Satyajit-babu was fairly liberal then with the editing of the score. There was a slight shortage of scoring for the scene where the itinerant sweet seller trudges in a certain rhythm with his wares and is trailed by the kids who cannot afford the treats. With the meend on the sitar and the "daw-o-o-o" drag of the ektara played by Subrata Mitra, the film's cinematographer, Satyajit-babu filled in the blank. All this was very much in my style. I had done similar things earlier in my compositions for my ballets *India Immortal* or *Discovery of India*. Satyajit-babu had liked them.

'Then awards and honours started coming his way. Thereafter, he started adjusting my scores, first in *Aparajito*, then in *Apur Sansar*. Even then the music of those films came out excellent...'

Ray's use of the word 'resent' and Shankar's application of the word 'adjust' are just two polite forms of addressing the same issue. Even before taking to composing for his films, Ray evidently was used to formulating his ideas fairly soon in the process—sometimes as early as in the scenario stage. And the final pleasure, of course, by his own admission, was in finding out that the music not only sounded good but also fit the scene for which it was meant. So, even the best musical compositions needed editing for a fine cut.

When I was interviewing Ravi Shankar in 1977—much of what went into *Smriti*—Satyajit Ray was yet to write his unique foreword to his collection of screenplays, *The Apu Trilogy*. That two-page foreword to the first edition of the volume in 1985 reads almost like a tribute to Ravi Shankar.

There he used the same word—'inspired'—as Shankar did to describe the magic realism of the theme music of *Pather Panchali*. Then he goes on to repeat the word for pieces conceived for *Aparajito* and *Apur Sansar*. The passage needs to be quoted verbatim:

'The main theme of *Pather Panchali*, usually heard on the bamboo flute, evolved in Ravi Shankar's mind even before he had seen the film. It was certainly a stroke of inspiration. Also inspired are certain musical motifs in the other two films. The Raga Jog is the basis of the melody which is heard in an impassioned outburst upon the death of Harihar in *Aparajito*. The same motif serves to suggest Sarbajaya's loneliness in the later stages of the film. Similarly inspired is the use of the poignant Raga Lachari Todi in *Apur Sansar* to represent the Apu-Aparna relationship.'

The tribute reaches a crescendo in the concluding paragraph of the foreword and I cannot resist quoting that as well:

'There is one scene in *Apur Sansar*, which is crucial from the point of view of music. It shows Apu's aimless wanderings after Aparna's death, and ends with him throwing away the manuscript of his novel in a gesture of renunciation. The music here, scored for flute and strings, has the noble simplicity of a Vedic hymn.'

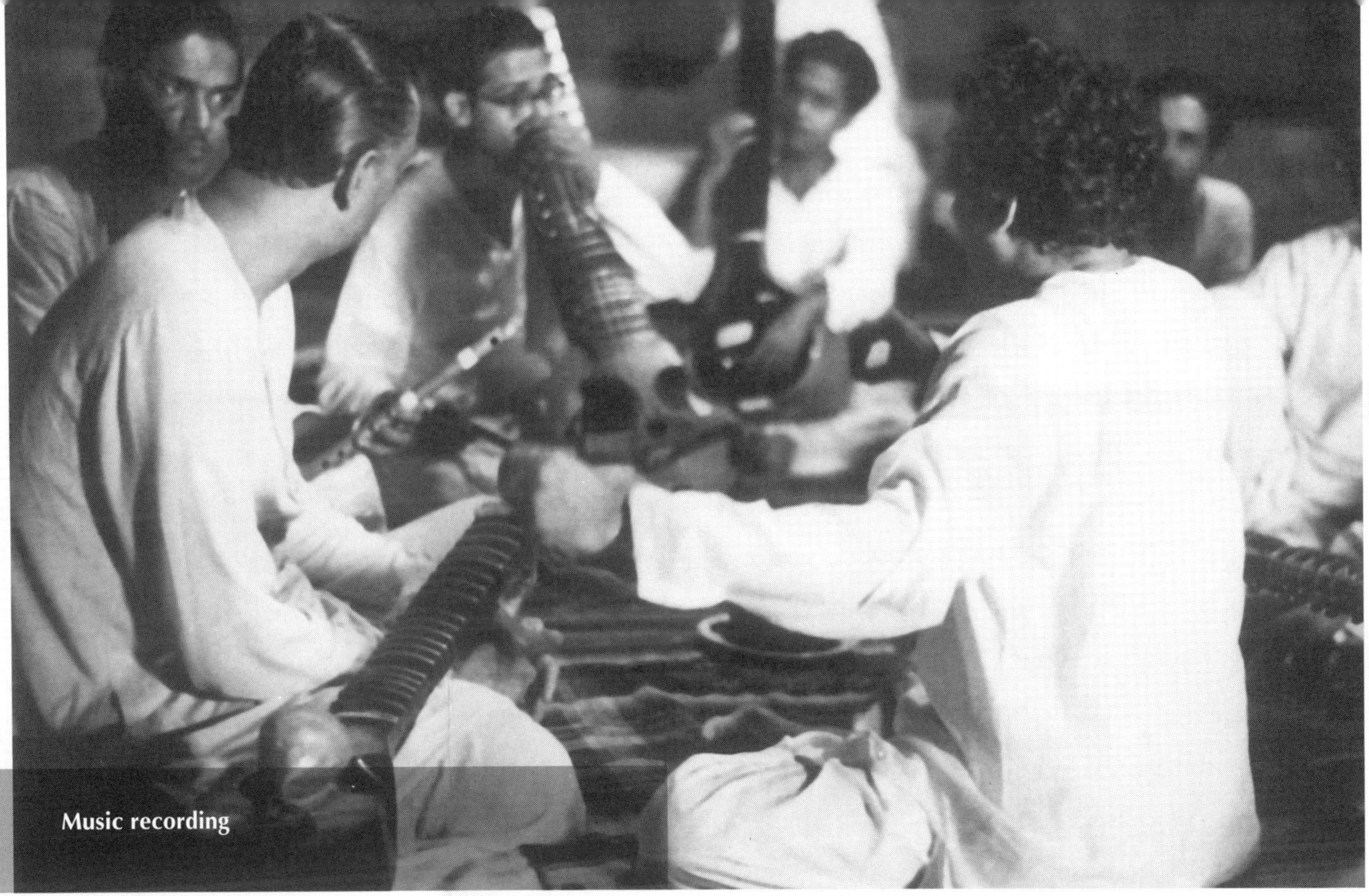

Music recording

When repeatedly reviewing the projected imagery of the alap and the madhya laya parts of the recital, one will be inclined to assume that the mood being invoked is sombre and poignant. The slow fall of dry leaves, the majestic massing clouds dissolving into images of the still water and a full-blown lotus—which then emerges as a detail of a lotus from a Rajput painting—all build up to the beautiful but brooding face of a maiden. With close-ups, dissolves and panning, Ray combines the details of the real lotus with a lotus petal carving on the banjaran guitar held by the maiden, her face reflecting a mood, a sentiment and, perhaps, a story of longing and separation. The alignment of the three lotuses in the eighteenth-century representation of the Ragini Todi—Ray's reference for the construction—languorously evolves into a sort of study of the three graces. This is unsurprising as they are associated with romance, but there is also a tinge of poignancy foreshadowing what the audiences were soon to experience in the relationship of the newly wedded Apu and Aparna in *Apur Sansar*, underscored by an inspired use of the Raga Lachari Todi on the sitar. The other unforgettable use of Todi in *The Apu Trilogy* is in *Pather Panchali* itself, in the sombre passage following Durga's death.

There is a strong argument in favour of Todi as

the raga of the recital by Ravi Shankar. But it does not explain two of the most decisive images of the album: the evening landscape and the storm. The argument for Desh, however, will be explained and discussed when we proceed to study the album as a script for a motion picture.

The two documentaries on living artists—Balasaraswati and Binode Bihari Mukherjee—that Satyajit Ray made later were markedly different in style from the unrealized *A Sitar Recital by Ravi Shankar*. *Bala*, the documentary on Balasaraswati, who according to Ray was 'the greatest Bharatanatyam dancer ever', was made ten years too late when Bala was fifty-eight, diabetic, and past her prime. His only consolation was that 'Bala filmed at fifty-eight was better than Bala not being filmed at all.' Though he could not portray Bala's early life, he utilized, for the duration of the film, an elaborate varnam that displays the astonishing range of an extraordinary performer. *The Inner Eye*, a searching study of the life, work and blindness of the artist Binode Bihari, travels in both space and time to explore the inner depths of the subject, his rearranged realities after the loss of his vision, and his understanding of his new state of being.

The documentary on Ravi Shankar is dissimilar to both these works—it is neither biographical nor operatic. Instead, it is a pure celebration of a genius artiste and the possibilities of a musical text. By the phrase 'possibilities of a musical text' is implied the delineation of images, the establishment of metaphors and the exploration of the emotional bandwidth. Film, like music, is a work of art which exists in time. *A Sitar Recital by Ravi Shankar* provided Ray with the novel scope for a movie on a concert—measure for measure, using the internal complexities of both music and cinema while surrendering nothing of their individual components, flair or grammar. Film-time and music-time being equal and the same, the music used in the film is actual music and the nucleus of the film. With this work we know cinema for what it is—to paraphrase Satyajit Ray himself—a language, an enormously potent and flexible language that can be used in just as many different ways as you can use the language of words.

A Sitar Recital by Ravi Shankar brings up the pertinent issue of adequacy: is such a film capable of adequately rendering on film the intricacies of a live performance? According to Siegfried Kracauer in his *Theory of Film*, it could be problematic or cinematic, depending on its function. He writes:

'It need hardly be stressed that films featuring music for its own sake are inconsistent with the medium. As we listen to a musical production number on the screen, we cannot help exchanging the dimension of outer impressions for that of inner sensations aroused by the inflowing rhythms and sound patterns—a shift of emphasis that evidently goes against the grain of film. We might as well do it in a concert hall. But are we really transformed into concertgoers? Interestingly, it is as if the spirit of the cinema interfered with the transformation. Imagine a film devoted to the reproduction of a concerto; imagine further that everything has been done to increase the impact of its rendition—camera activities are reduced to a minimum and the visuals never try to create diversions. Under these favourable circumstances, we should, in principle, be in a position to enjoy undisturbedly the beauty of the concert and its peculiar significance. Yet this is not what actually happens.

'When during a musical performance in a film the camera ceases to move—like a concertgoer who forgets to breathe because of his involvement in the score—the ensuing loss of pictorial life does not as a rule benefit our responsiveness as listeners but, on the contrary, makes us feel uneasy about the design behind the whole performance; it is as though life had gone out of the music also. With camera-reality being subdued, music, however perfectly executed, affects us as something that does not belong—a protracted intrusion rather than a crowning achievement. The result is ennui, provided the moviegoer in us does not deliberately surrender to the concertgoer. But this would be an act of resignation.'

Ray's documentary requires no surrender of the moviegoer to the concertgoer; its camera activity is in no way reduced, though its visuals, interestingly, never attempt to create diversions. All the extra-stage visuals are self-reflexive and take their meaning from the music played and subsequently add their own freight of signs, colours, images and aromas to the central musical text. There is no loss of pictorial life even when Ray's camera focuses on Ravi Shankar and ceases to move, because the intense, youthful, artistic face of the maestro is as much a part of the design behind the whole performance, and there is no reason to suspect that the camera-reality has been subdued. From the very first shots, the documentary reveals the director's love affair with the subject's face and the message, structure and appeal of the raga. The film, though dedicated to a concert, does not quite feature music for its own sake and, therefore, is not inconsistent with the medium. However, as it is lacking in speech or commentary, it has music for its tongue, and as the text unfolds, it may be gradually perceived as a dialogic interplay between the sitar and the camera.

Ray, who possessed from the beginning of his career his own theory regarding the formal weakness of Indian films, felt Indian directors tended to overlook the musical aspect of a film's structure. He had argued in his 1965 essay 'Film Making':

'The reason lies surely in the absence of a dramatic narrative tradition in Indian music ... Western classical music underwent a process of humanization with the invention of the sonata form—with its masculine first subjects and feminine second subjects and their interweaving and progress through a series of dramatic key-changes, to a point of culmination.

'But a raga is a raga—with a single predetermined mood and tonality—that is built up like a temple, starting from a solid base of alap, culminating in a spire of flourishes on the higher octaves of the scale. Perhaps one could, with some stretch of imagination, think of a film subject that might be built up like the development of a raga, but I cannot think of this as a form with wide application.'

By 'wide application' Ray was referring to the vast majority of the stories that provided the material for our films, which could be told in a style that had already found universal application—the style, Ray says, which had originated in Hollywood. With *Pather Panchali*, Ray had already broken away from that style—his feature film was lauded as a human document without parallel, at least in Indian cinema. *A Sitar Recital by Ravi Shankar* was, to begin with, a documentary with yet another critical sense of form and a rhythmic pattern existing in time. The broad aspects of the film's rhythm, as Ray had imagined it, are already contained in the scenario. All the developments of mood, tonality, texture and so on are provided by the various elements that come into play as the music progresses. For a change, even by Ray's shibboleth, a film is conceived and executed in the manner of an alap, jor and jhala, and instead of being a sequence of dramatic key-changes or upheavals, grows from the base upwards, like a temple.

Ray had called the script of the Ravi Shankar recital a rough sketch. Although extensively laid out, almost shot by shot, it was perhaps only a core design that could develop into any manner of visual composition, depending on the unfurling of the musical text. Though never turned into a movie, *A Sitar Recital by Ravi Shankar* easily invites comparative study with two great documentaries on art forms if only because of its approach to the documentary trend. The first, Duvivier's *The Great Waltz*, shows Johann Strauss composing his '*Tales from the Vienna Woods*', concentrating on the genesis of a work rather than the work itself. Kracauer, in his magisterial exposition of the principle, argues thus:

'Since the finished work lends itself to being rendered on the screen only in as much as the cinema is also a reproduction technique, the film-maker prefers to present the work not as it is but as it becomes; in other words, he has us witness the creative processes from which it arises. In picturing the pre-natal stages of a painting, he lures it back into the very dimension which is the camera's hunting ground.'

Ray's film is a detailed study of a creative process, the step-by-step elaboration of a raga that eventually becomes a musical text. The procedure is strikingly illustrated in another great documentary on the art process, Henri-Georges Clouzot's *The Mystery of Picasso*, where the camera is often placed behind the translucent canvas on which the artist is painting, faithfully recording his activities. As viewers of the film, we are accorded a seat behind the canvas and are witnesses to the act of creation. Kracauer describes it as a most exciting spectacle.

Ray's documentary too works on a similar principle of spectacle—the maestro's finger on the fret, exploring the colours of the raga, framing permutations and combinations of notes, sliding down octaves to reach a specific swar, or rising up in a spire of flourishes on the higher octaves of the scale. The film, while capturing the flitting moments of the sound, also reproduces for the viewer the technique of playing the sitar and the process of achieving artistry. *A Sitar Recital by Ravi Shankar,* at a certain level, separates the moviegoer from the concertgoer, allowing him the freedom to enjoy a unique concert as a spectacle, combining in his head the pleasures of the ear with the pleasures of the eye to create a unified cinematic experience.

Does Ray, in *A Sitar Recital by Ravi Shankar,* like Clouzot in *The Mystery of Picasso,* invent a style of arresting the movement of the respective artistic process he is filming? In Clouzot's film, the occasional cigarette breaks, the intervening interviews and Picasso's interaction with the director, even as he continues applying the brush to the canvas, are all part of an activity associated with painting, and the camera seems to develop a style of painting the artist as he paints. Ray's camera languidly, and in harmony with the meditative pace of the alap, acquires the nature and quality of a musical instrument playing in consonance with the music on screen. Technically, it might sound like a revelation, but artistically that is what it appears to be. For the moment, we will only consider the elegant and speechless introduction of the alap.

Going by the album, the title card simply reads in one frame—*A Sitar Recital by Ravi Shankar*. We do not know if it is accompanied by a warm-up chikari. The following frame is once again a solid dark screen, evidently the concert stage waiting to break into light, with the silhouette of Ravi Shankar positioned against a halogenic arc resembling a rising sun. It is possible that Ray was playing on the maestro's name, as Ravi means the sun. This is not an unlikely conclusion since, when mulling over a picture for Aloke Mitra's photographic album on Ravi Shankar, Ray had picked up a shot showing Ravi Shankar with his sitar on a bajra, floating on the Ganga in Benares, with the rising sun hovering right behind his head. Having settled on the image, he told Aloke almost as an aside, 'Now the name suitably goes with the image, Ravi and Ravi!'

Once Ravi Shankar is revealed on stage with the camera at a distance, the tracking forward begins—gradually revealing more of Ravi and developing further the arc of light as a representation of sunrise. The tracking continues in the manner of a meend, the slow, heavy, resonant sliding from note to note, connecting the sounds using srutis, expressing gradually the details and gravitas of the artiste and image—the picture of the artiste and the raga start to gel.

All this is in the alap, the introductory phase of the raga, which expresses and then unfolds its characteristics. The meticulously planned tracking and the extensive panning that are to follow serve also as alap or an initial conversation with the maestro. Alap, in its common usage, refers to 'getting acquainted'. Ray's camera slides from image to image like his subject's fingers shift from string to string to bring out microtones, his camera-play working on approaching or receding from the image.

At the end of the tracking, Ray remains focused on Ravi Shankar, full screen, in a majestic study, and then pans further and further away to reduce the image, slowly moving away from the stage to eventually leave a blank, well-lit stage with nothing more than the platform visible. This again is a trick. By this point, the emergent platform—the dais—appears to be a distant playing ground. Ray dissolves the shot into one of an evening countryside landscape, complete with a flock of homing birds. The dais becomes the base of the image—the land or desh? The desh, as land or motherland, translates into Desh as raga in Ray's film and frequently reminds us of the three-minute solo sitar piece by Ravi Shankar in *Pather Panchali*.

Two sequences in *Pather Panchali*, both virtually wordless, were conceived in terms of music. One was the sequence of the rain and the other the long episode with Apu, after the death of Durga. For the sombre passage following Durga's death, the raga used was Todi, while for the extremely lyrical passage showing Durga dancing soulfully in the rain, thereafter to tragically fall sick and die, Raga Desh, conventionally associated with rain, was chosen. With the surrounding imagery imagined by Ray, *A Sitar Recital by Ravi Shankar* appears to almost take off from the last happy scene in, by then, the two-year-old classic. The music that we hear after the scintillating Desh is the sombre Todi, and the utterly heartbreaking Patdeep, played on the dilruba in the upper reaches, when Harihar brings out the sari for Durga and her mother Sarbajaya collapses in a flood of tears.

The release, both visual and musical, comes at the end when Harihar and his family leave their small plot of land, uprooted from their desh so to speak, and depart by bullock cart as the airy, liberating tune of the theme music comes back on screen.

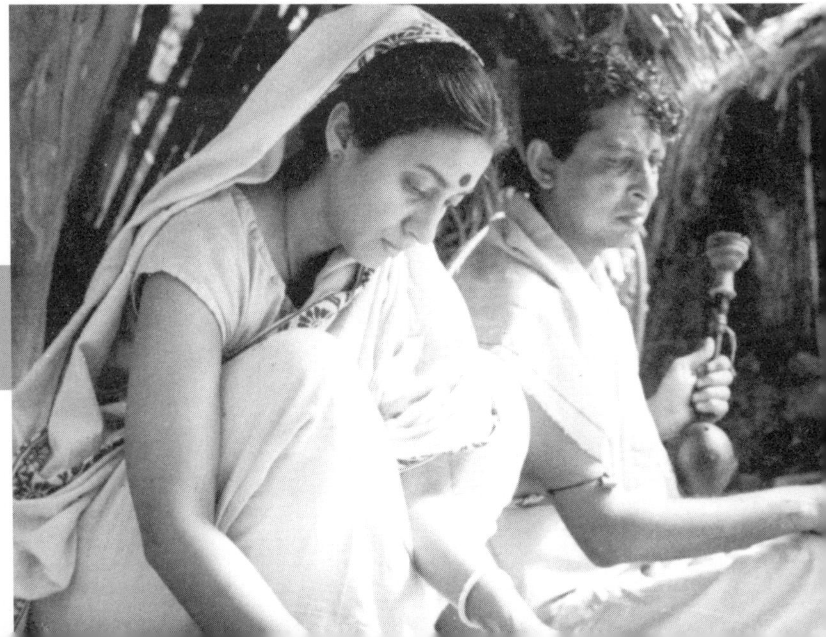

Sarbajaya and Harihar in *Pather Panchali*

To connoisseurs of *Pather Panchali*, the elaboration of Desh in *A Sitar Recital by Ravi Shankar* would have been an evocation of the sight, soil and soul of Nischindipur, the desh of Harihar, Sarbajaya, Apu and Durga.

Unfortunately, I wasn't fully aware of how extensively Satyajit Ray had worked on the Ravi Shankar documentary and therefore did not often bring up the issue in the several interviews I had with him dating from the end of the 1970s to end-January 1992, just before he was hospitalized for the last time. It is even more upsetting that just when he had given me permission to conduct interviews for his memoir in Bengali, in the style of *Raag-Anuraag* (Ravi Shankar's autobiography as told to me), his health began deteriorating. The ABP Group, the sole publishers of all of Ray's books in Bangla and *Raag-Anuraag*, wanted me to collaborate with Ray on a similar project and had, accordingly, obtained his permission for the project. Ray had wanted me to provide approximately twenty-five basic questions to enable him to figure out my plan and approach. In sheer excitement I prepared many more and handed him the sheaf of papers one evening. He promptly looked through a few pages and said with a smile, 'Aamaar lekha sab pore felechho dekhchhi' (It seems you have read all my writings).

Later that evening, he called my bosses at ABP—Aveek and Arup Sarkar—to express his satisfaction with my plan and to grant his approval to the project. Soon after we began planning dates he turned up one evening at Ananda Shankar's newly built bungalow on Palm Avenue for a housewarming party where Ravi Shankar was to perform a glorious Mohan Kauns. Ray went home that evening in high spirits and full of praise for both Ravi Shankar's rendering and the structuring of the raga he had created on Mahatma Gandhi's death. Then a music producer with Akashvani, Delhi, Ravi Shankar had been asked to play in memory of Gandhiji on the anniversary of his martyrdom. In a fit of inspiration, Ravi Shankar worked on the notes Ga Ni Dha, picking the sounds from the name Gandhi, and set them in Kauns ang, naming it Mohan Kauns as a tribute to Mohandas Karamchand.

That very night Ray fell sick, suffering from a lack of equilibrium in his auditory system. This caused him to be admitted to hospital for the first time and over the next ten years, he had to be repeatedly hospitalized, resulting in the planned memoir being indefinitely postponed. The last time I interviewed him, he very touchingly said, 'I can now feel a Bengali book growing in me. Just let me get up and round this ailment, and we'll do it.'

He was taken to hospital after a day or two and that was the last the world saw of him.

Amidst the scores of questions I had handed to him that evening, years before, were enquiries on the Ravi Shankar documentary. Would that have inspired him to shoot the film? I'm not sure, especially since Ravi Shankar had by then aged so much. However, I soon had occasion, after his first stroke, to glimpse how strong his admiration for Ravi Shankar still was.

Before one of his trips to Kolkata, Ravi Shankar had enquired about Ray's health. When told that he was recovering gradually, Ravi Shankar wanted to know if he could drop by to see him. I had asked Nemai Ghosh, Ray's photo-biographer, to find out and was soon told that he would be happy if Ravi Shankar dropped in. Accordingly, one wintry morning, I escorted Ravi Shankar from the airport to Subhash Ghosal's place in the Hastings area by the Hooghly. Ghosal, an influential figure in the field of advertising and a friend of Ray's, had offered his bungalow to the director for a quiet convalescence. I still remember the excellent adda that ensued over tea and snacks when the maestro turned up at the auteur's getaway. Soumitra Chatterjee, incidentally, was also visiting Ray and found an added bonus in meeting Ravi Shankar. He was puffing away at a pipe Ray had apparently

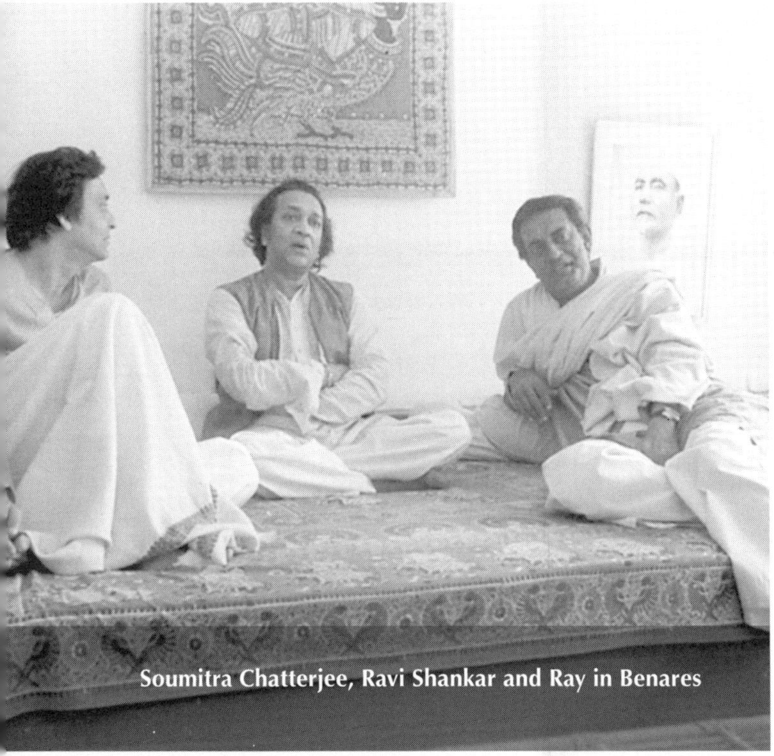
Soumitra Chatterjee, Ravi Shankar and Ray in Benares

gifted him after quitting smoking himself. Pointing at him, Ravi Shankar joked, 'Now he's taken over where he (Ray) had left off.' When Ray was seeing him off, he said, 'Hope to come to your concert next time. This time I have to let it go.' At that point Ravi Shankar joked again, 'Can I forget you had that ear problem after my recital at Ananda's?' They both burst out in laughter as Ray professed, 'No, no, we can't allow that to be repeated.'

In the car, Ravi Shankar started reminiscing about his association with Ray in the 1950s and recounted how the director had recently reacted to the ten-volume long-play album he had scripted and prepared as an introduction to Indian classical music. Ravi Shankar had not only played his instrument but had also sung the dhrupad numbers to illustrate the initial phases of Indian classical music. Listening to his dhrupad vocals, Ray had reportedly told some of his associates excitedly, 'Ki tomra Ravi Shankar-er setar-setar karo, shono lokta ki gaye.' (You always go ga-ga over Ravi Shankar's sitar, now listen to this and discover what an excellent singer he is.) Ravi Shankar then touched his forehead and said, 'Let him get over this quickly. He has so much left to offer.'

For a good ten years it had been my job to convey reports of Ray's health and work to Ravi Shankar and vice versa. On his trip to India after a major heart surgery in New York, Ravi Shankar seemed extremely excited over his new-found good health and minutely described the process, finally capping it with the statement, 'It was really nice to receive a phone call from Manik-babu.' Ravi Shankar too, I remembered, was in constant communication with the hospital when Ray was undergoing his cardiac surgery in the US.

Coincidentally, ABP gave me the task of meeting Ravi Shankar in New Delhi to get him to speak on Ray for an obituary piece. However, Ray had not yet been pronounced dead though the doctors had given up all hope. When I described to Ravi Shankar the actual situation, he raised his brows and exclaimed, 'What? The man is still alive and you want me to speak on him as if he were dead? Isn't it the business of vultures?' I agreed and said, 'But that's how the media runs. Your copy will be designed and ready for whenever the sad event occurs.' Ravi Shankar kept silent for a while, presumably recalling the bygone days and then, suddenly, started to speak. I cannot forget the words with which he eventually rounded up the piece. He said what he admired most in Satyajit was his deep foothold in the Indian soil and reality even as he stretched out to reach the world abroad. 'The reason why Satyajit, the artist, is important to me is that he is out and out a Bengali and an Indian while being intensely international,' he said. He then went on:

'He has a sense of the world and a worldview, an approach towards the universal. The way the scenes, characters, story and tunes of *Pather Panchali* belong to the world in spite of their being rooted in a village in Bengal is something you found in Rabindranath, in dada (Uday Shankar). Like them, Satyajit's power to emerge as an international force lies there. I have always adored Tagore's attitude of standing firm on his native ground while testing the boundaries of space and time. I have adored this in dada, and I should say in Satyajit too. This worldview of theirs has always been my inspiration.'

Before moving into the details of the script on Ravi Shankar, I will digress once more to narrate an anecdote related by Ray himself in which they both feature. It is present in his extremely witty newspaper account of the failed attempt at filming his English script *The Alien*, which appeared in the Kolkata *Statesman* in 1980. An unsavoury character named Mike Wilson had flown Ray to Los Angeles to strike a deal with Columbia Pictures for *The Alien*. Peter Sellers, meanwhile, had agreed to play a part in the film. By sheer coincidence, he too was in Los Angeles to act in another film in which he portrayed an Indian character who also played the sitar. Ray and Sellers had met earlier in Paris, where a special screening of *Charulata* was arranged to enable him to form an impression of Ray's style. At the end of this screening, a red-eyed Sellers had turned to Ray and said, 'Why do you need me? I'm not better than your actors, you know!' The two met again soon enough in Los Angeles, and that too at Ravi Shankar's home! Ray describes this meeting in 'Ordeals of the Alien' as follows:

'The first meeting with Sellers was at Ravi Shankar's place. The Indian part in the new comedy called for his going through the motion of playing the sitar, and Sellers was anxious to get his fingering right. Ravi Shankar had promised to play after dinner. With simple Bengali dishes backed by superb north Indian contributions from Ravi Shankar's gifted accompanist Alla Rakha, the dinner was an unqualified success. During the splendid recital that followed, Sellers sat cross-legged on the carpet, intently watchful, and simulated learned response by judicious interjections of wah-wahs.'

From this image of Ravi Shankar and Alla Rakha playing to an invited crowd at the former's residence at Los Angeles, we can cut to the concert stage of *A Sitar Recital by Ravi Shankar*. Some ten-odd years back in time, from an ostensibly happy hour in a foreign land to an introspective invocation of Desh or motherland and monsoon. Alla Rakha was not his accompanist then; could the fingers on the table then be of Chaturlal? Perhaps, but in Ray's sketched-out scenario, we do not see the face. We return to the only face we see ... through a lens, darkly.

A Sitar Recital by Ravi Shankar opens with a silhouetted image of Ravi Shankar in the long view to which the camera zooms in. The tracking ends at the full-screen image of the maestro, which the camera holds for a while before panning away. The film ends with the camera tracking further back from a shot of the maestro, held steady and bright, after a series of swings in the first tempo segment of the recital. The tracking back gradually reduces the image of the subject to the silhouette of the first long shot with which the film had begun. In compliance with the circle-like image of an Indian raga performance, Ray's nearly musical visual rendering of a concert virtually comes full circle. The arc of light in the backdrop, which expands in the opening shots as a sunrise, recedes in the end like a sunset. But both are caught in that period when evening merges into the first quarter of the night.

Why conclude that it is an evening raga? This is because, as has been shown earlier in this essay, Ray's camera pans away from the first images of the recital into an evening landscape. It is the only visual mention of a specific time in the script. The introduction of a Rajput painting delineating Ragini Todi is, after all, in reference to a motif of a lotus and the face of a maiden that resembles a lotus. The dark formation of clouds and the screaming winds passing through dales, waterbodies and meadows bring to mind the unforgettable image of rain and storm in *Pather Panchali*. Unlike in Bibhuti Bhushan Bandyopadhyay's description of the storm as a dark and terrifying movement of nature in the famous Bildungsroman, Ray's description of the storm in *Pather Panchali*, despite its force and ferocity, has a certain joy and freedom about it. Coming after days of sultry heat, it thrills Durga to the bones and draws her out into the open fields. For her, it

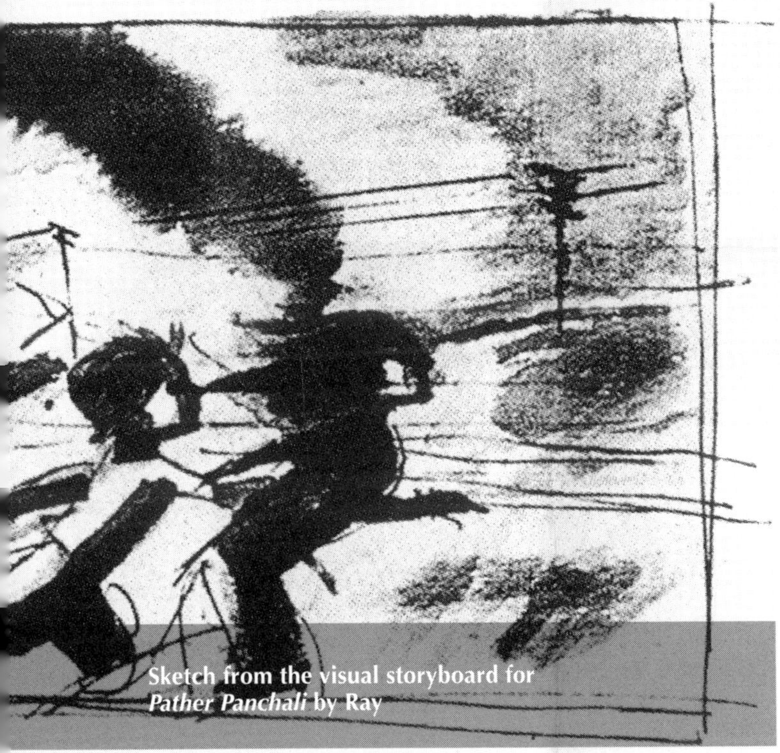

Sketch from the visual storyboard for *Pather Panchali* by Ray

is symbolic of music and merriment, never hinting at the fatal illness that was to follow. Mainly to promote this joi de vivre, Ravi Shankar chose Desh as the background melody instead of a more sombre one, for example, Malhar. Even the three-minute solo sitar Desh that Ravi Shankar applies is in a faster tempo to match the fluid camera, taking in the thrill and romance of the rain. It is the depth and lyricism of Desh that was pivotal to the drama and irony of the scene in the rain. The sounds of the strings plucked and fingered by Ravi Shankar in the rhythmic mode of dance had a liquid flair and an air of levitation—a subtle composite of seriousness and mirth. The manner in which the music reflects the visuals creates a choreography that positions this sequence as a central piece in the film—one that evokes what has already happened and what is to follow thereafter. Desh, indicating monsoon, keeps the characters waiting for Sarat and Hemanta, two fleeting periods in autumn that will bring better times, the festival of Durga Puja, and Harihar's return.

Like *Pather Panchali*, the Ravi Shankar documentary too has a plethora of images of nature ranging from the slow passage of clouds to the stillness of water in the ponds and the lotus blooming therein. Assuming the raga played is Desh, the finger on the fret rests on the note Re—the prominent note of the raga—making it central to the melody. The meend from Ma to Re via Ga is also one of the vital features in the raga, and that is the image into which the images of nature finally dissolve. Ray situates this visual as the pinnacle of the short alap segment, cutting from this, with a change of lighting, to the vilamvit gat. From the image of the meend to the vilamvit gat or the slow rhythmic cycle, Ray uses a track forward shot before cutting to the image with altered lighting. This implies a fair amount of alap development in the interim; after all, the album is a rough sketch of how the camera will behave while the music is on. In other words, the sketches are photographic freezes of the fluid passage of the camera. The gat, incidentally, brings the first cut in the filming from the initial camerawork of tracking, panning and dissolving. The cut sets in motion further cuts, camera slants, zooms and more tracking and dissolves in different lighting, all in a rhythmic motion, however slow in speed.

Ray uses one swing of the camera to move from the sitar to the tabla with only the hands of the accompanist shown, and then he tracks his camera back to have the sitarist in full view and the tabla revealed from the right edge of the frame. He then continues to a further cut to capture the full figure of Ravi Shankar.

Due to the slow interplay of strings and drum in the slow-cycle segment, Ray plays his camera to various cuts before entering into slants. The slants, of course, are a preparation for a change of speed and a passage towards newer imagery—in this case, decorating panels. The final slant of the vilamvit gat gets the sitar in a clean horizontal position and dissolves into a relief sculpture panel, which again is replaced by several more panels, all as a result of the influence of cuts. The swift cuts enjoin speed to the flow, and the selection of the successive panels is also made in a way that ensures that the decorations themselves suggest speed. From floral patterns, the cuts lead the viewers to three sculptures of feminine faces which probably complement the mood of the melody more than the rhythm. They are also possibly introduced to the screen to eventually lead to the camera zooming down on the tabla on the concert stage.

Even in this zoom-down on the tabla, the percussionist is absent. In all the movements, all we see of him are the two playing hands. Is it all because Ray had not yet decided on the instrumentalist or because his concept of the documentary circled around just the overwhelming image of the maestro? The latter of the two possibilities seems stronger to me as I study the script and also recall what Ray had once told me regarding his attitude to documentaries on personalities, living or dead. In response to my query regarding possible future documentaries, Ray had said, 'The first requirement is the stature of the subject concerned. You need to have respect and admiration for the person you intend to work on. Where do you find a personality like that?'

There is a further argument in favour of Ray deciding to focus on the lone image of Ravi Shankar for the film. He did not see the film as simply a recital where the accompanist was an integral presence. The recital was also a journey of exploration, from a concert into the concepts of melody, nature, man and art. Ravi Shankar, I remember, had told me, 'Satyajit-babu wanted to use my curly shock of hair as a pattern to launch out from, into the leaves of trees and floating clouds. He also wanted to see the melodies of the sitar as curled lines rising upwards into the air.' This imagery of a concert cannot permit the distraction of a second human presence. Besides, the god-given charm and beauty of the face of Ravi Shankar demanded a study in isolation.

The zoom-down from the sculpture of a female face to the daina-baya of the tabla is interesting. From the decoration panels the camera first cuts to the face whose eyes are closed and which is tilted slightly downwards. The left cut brings the same face leaning to the left with the eyes closed. A further cut conveys an image of the woman looking upwards with her eyes possibly open. The eyes of this frame suggest another pair of dots looking out of the dark space of the following frame. The solid dark circles in the middle of the white spaces of the tabla are like the irises of a pair of eyes looking out of a dark faceless visage. From that image the camera moves down to several perspectives of the tabla with a pair of hands playing it. The final frame brings up a close shot of the tabla and the hands, only to cut to a stark image of the sitar—no player and no fingers—spread across the frame at approximately a fifty-degree angle from the base, with the two globular pieces (the lau and the tumba) at both ends of the instrument vaguely simulating the rounded pieces of the tabla. Then the camera zooms forward to get an expanded view of the sitar, followed by a look at the instrument, at which point both hands of the performer appear. Thus the camera's transition from the tabla to the sitar is, in other words, a progression from a study of circular images to a study of a vertical linear image. From the solo image of the sitar the camera then draws back to grab both the instruments in a top shot, cuts once more to the tabla and lowers itself down to the level of the pieces, and eventually to the base of the drums.

Despite being cut-and-zoom scenes they retain so much of the fluidity of the initial phases that they serve as a vibrant narrative of the flow of music. The conversation of the instrument is held by cut-to-cut shots in the middle tempo, leading to a passage of druta laya or fast tempo and engaging with the imagery of the storm. Here the speed of the fingers on the fret and the sitar held horizontally invoke the storm whirling through the skies, over the water-bodies and the farmlands or meadows. From the meadows and the flowers of the fields, Ray cuts back to the plucking fingers of Ravi Shankar that are furiously working on the strings to drum up speed. There is a storm on the strings that calls for a cut to the frame of the tabla to actually illustrate the mounting speed. That introduces the fast tempo conversation resulting in sath sangat or joint play and at times—because the performer is Ravi Shankar who popularized the specific ang or craft—the sawal-jawab or question and answer.

The low-angle shot that Ray now selects to accentuate the image of the artiste in a state of heightened physical and mental activity takes in for the first time the figure of the tabla artiste far out to the right. This is mainly to balance the inflated image of the base or globular part of the sitar, the lau, with the image of the percussionist with his drums, and also to create the visual option of a top shot and film the sitarist and his sitar from an angle previously not used.

Fans and admirers of Ravi Shankar will easily recollect that the low-angle and top shots of the maestro are also iconic images of him, popularized by the photos on the covers of his albums. The other famous image of Ravi Shankar, clasping his sitar as if feeling the vibes of his strings, probably the most celebrated of his performance photos, takes over from the high and low shots to achieve a centrality of image. This is followed by the central image of the fingers traversing octaves on the instrument, at a heightened tempo, closing in on the pinnacle of speed or jhala.

With the music speed reaching a peak, the camera too attempts a flourish. And what better way to imbibe the spirit of the music than to repeatedly swing? Which is what the camera does, first swinging upwards and then, with each swing closing in on a more detailed image of the sitarist, downwards but still closing in till Ravi Shankar fills the entire screen. The camera then holds him.

This is when the lighting changes, ushering in a new drama of sight and sound. The camera then begins to track back. The image here is almost exactly the one the camera had tracked forward to and held in the alap stage, before panning away from the concert stage and into nature. Now the track back gently reduces the image of the artiste and allows the backlighting to resurface, gradually resembling the setting of the sun—ravi—behind another Ravi, now cautiously bringing his recital to its denouement. When the sound fades away, a solid dark frame takes over, this time with the message 'The End' and possibly accompanied by a resounding chikari.

I feel that it is apt to conclude this essay with another Ray-Ravi anecdote. It was the morning after Ravi Shankar's recital at Ananda Shankar's. I was at Lala Sridhar's residence on Ballygunge Park Road where Ravi Shankar was staying. With me was the chief executive of Ananda Publishers, Dwijendranath Basu, better known as Badal Basu. For him it was both a courtesy and a professional visit. After a few exchanges over *Raag-Anuraag*, the conversation veered first to the recital the previous evening and then to Satyajit Ray. Ravi Shankar was extremely happy that Ray could make it and that he had enjoyed the performance so much. Then Badal-babu reported what had happened to Ray late the previous night. Almost instantly, Ravi Shankar's mood changed and he fell silent for a while. Finally he said, 'What a sad turn to such a lovely evening!'

After some time he turned to me and continued, 'Know what? Before I came to Kolkata I had chanced to see a Bombay newspaper once again raking up that old issue of Manik-babu and me falling out over the editing of some of my music for *Aparajito* and *Apur Sansar*. I couldn't help wondering why all this all over again! But it evaporated when I saw him at the concert. Now the report of his illness makes the heart heavy.'

Ray was bedridden for quite some time that year. Badal-babu, a regular visitor to Ray's drawing room on professional matters, had apparently told him of our conversation with Ravi Shankar at Lala Sridhar's place. When Ravi Shankar next came to Kolkata the following winter and Badal-babu went with me to meet him, he smilingly mentioned, 'You see, Manik-babu wrote me a nice letter explaining that the article in the Bombay journal was very much a desk job and he had not given them any interview for the same. He urged me not to give it any importance and to leave it all behind. And that's precisely what I'm going to do. It was barely on my mind for so long, you know that, Sankar. Now tell me how is Manik-babu?' Badal-babu once again quoted Ravi Shankar's comments to Ray who, on learning this, had reportedly exclaimed, 'So he's got the letter? Oh, what a relief!'

Ray and Ravi were falling sick in turns hereafter and could rarely meet. I had a whole set of questions for Ray on Ravi Shankar, for his Bengali memoirs which eventually did not materialize. On the contrary, I was to meet Ravi Shankar for an obituary article in Delhi when his friend lay dying in hospital in Kolkata. Apart from that obituary Ravi Shankar was to compose a far superior tribute to Satyajit Ray in the form of a sitar recital recording entitled *Farewell My Friend*. It was a superb rendering of the Raga Rajya Kalyan, followed by variations on the theme of *Pather Panchali*. The reason for the evocation of *Pather Panchali* is obvious, but Rajya Kalyan—as the very name suggests—was conceived and executed as a royal tribute to a very regal personality.

Rough Sketches
for a film of

A SITAR RECITAL

BY

Ravishankar

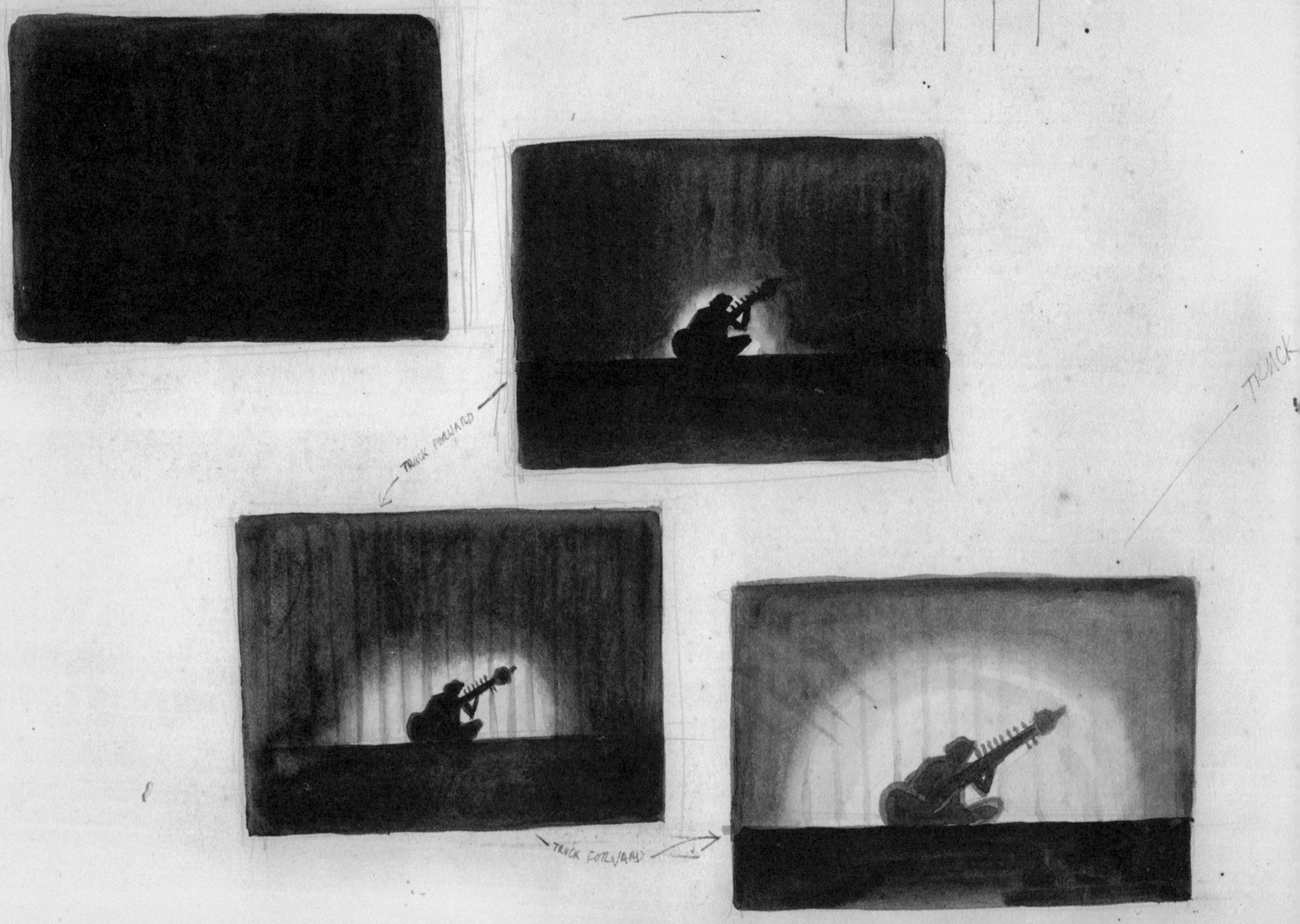
TRUCK FORWARD
TRUCK FORWARD
TRUCK

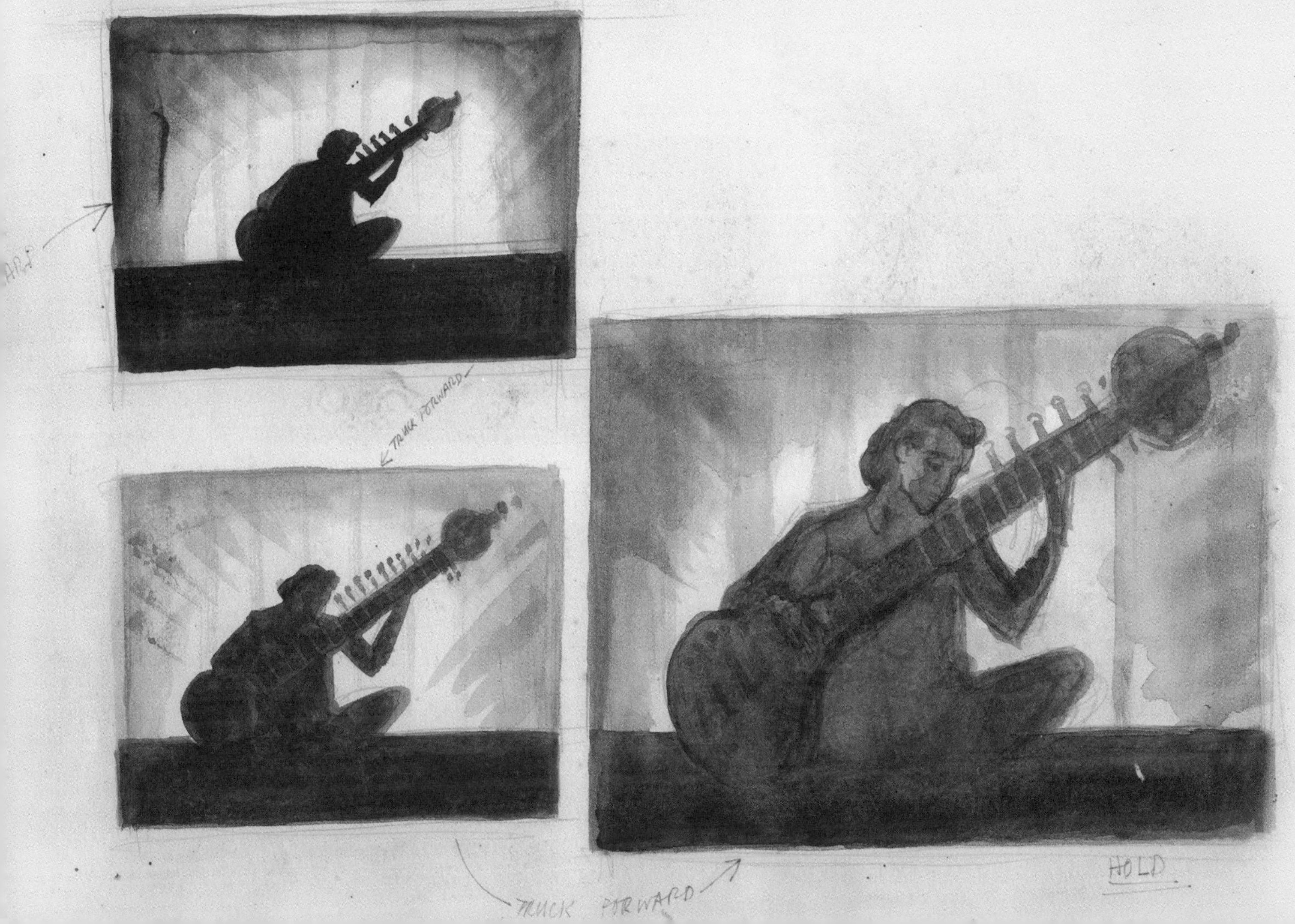
TRUCK FORWARD
TRUCK FORWARD
HOLD

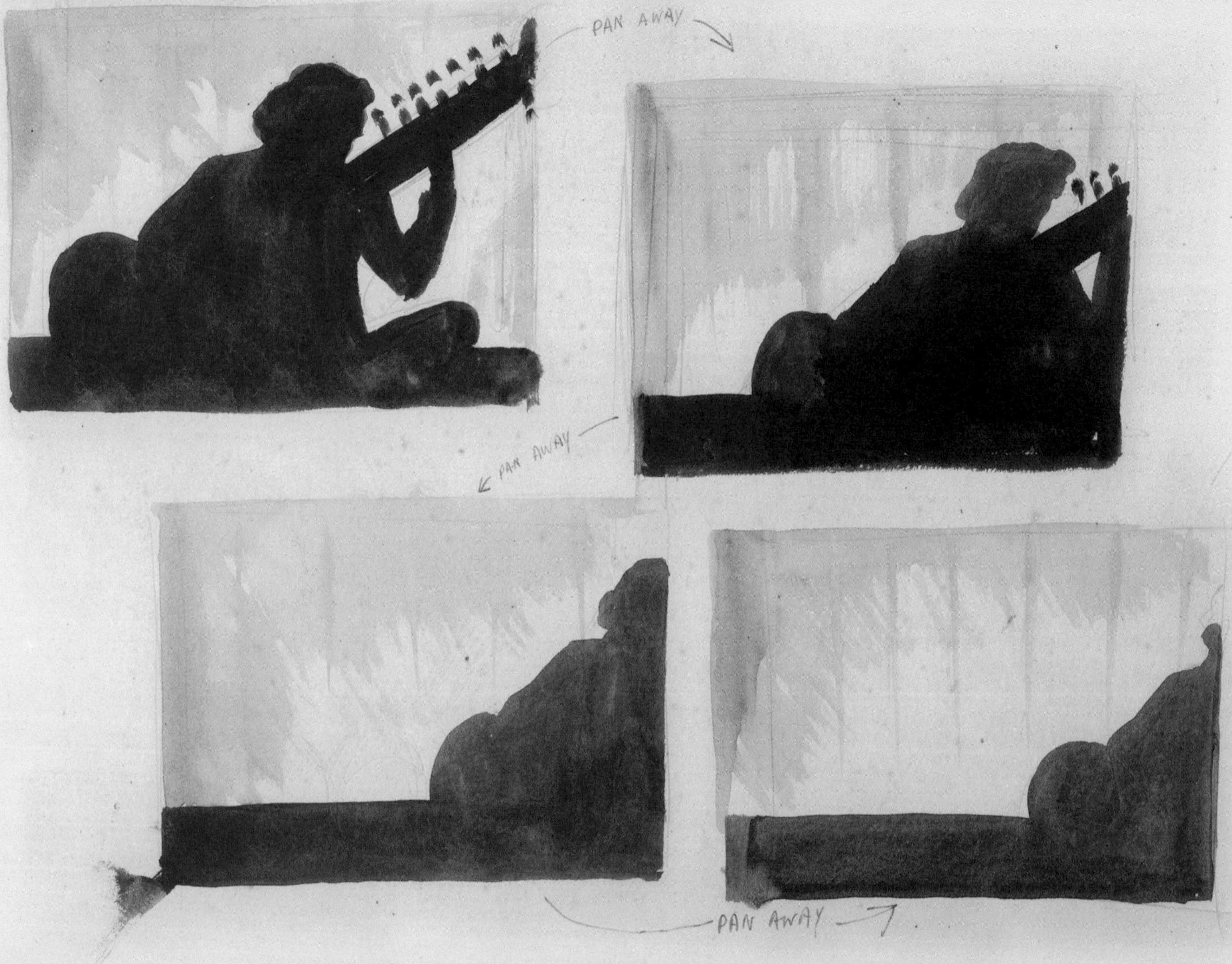
PAN AWAY
PAN AWAY
PAN AWAY

PAN AWAY →

PLATFORM

DISSOLVE TO →

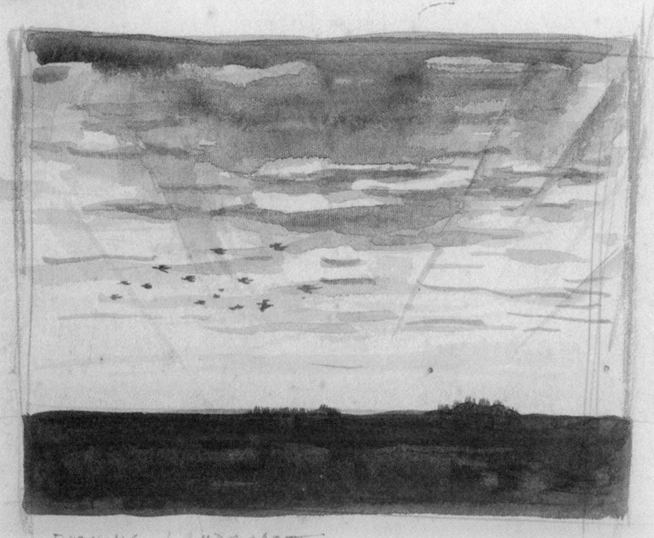

BURNING LANDSCAPE

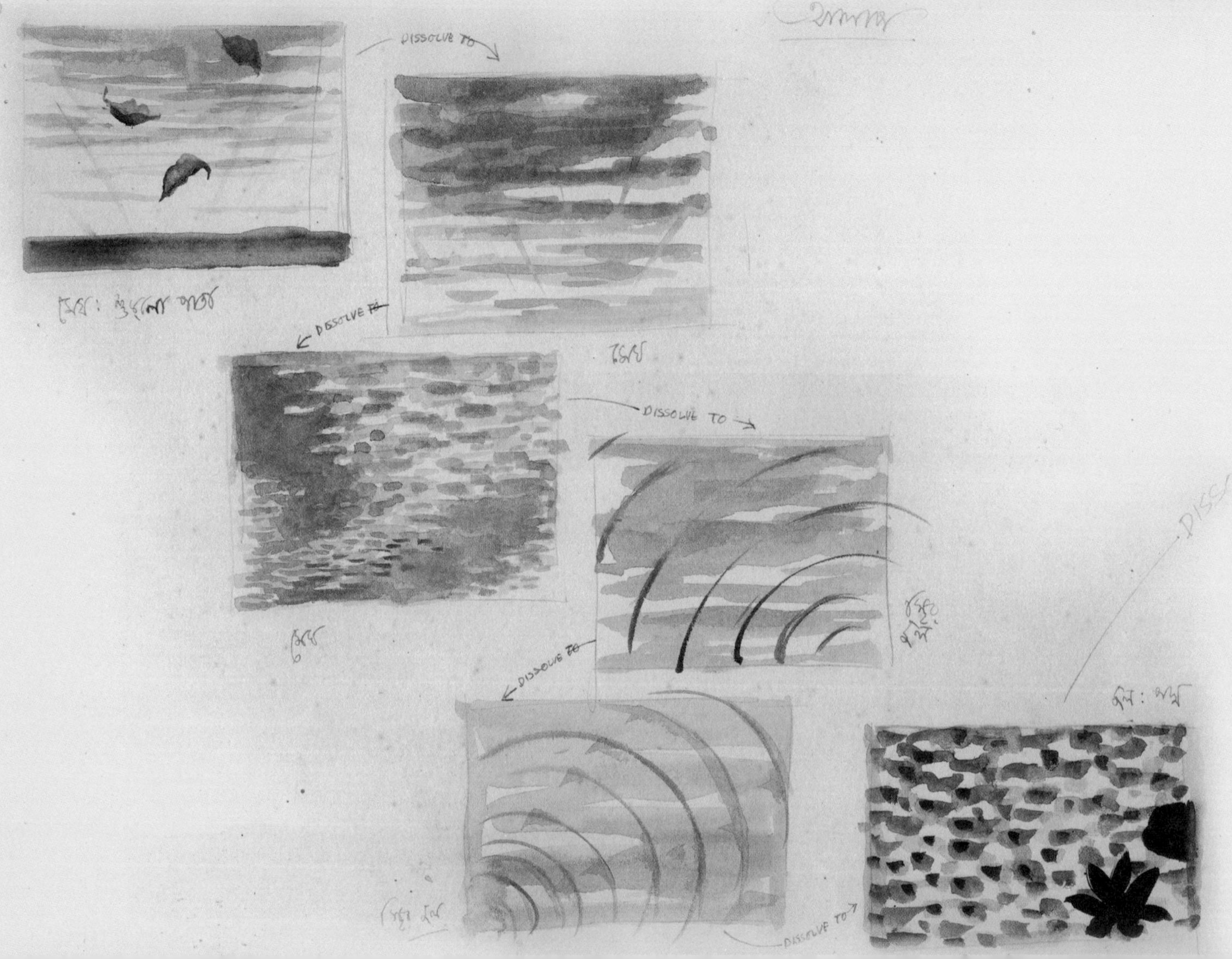
DISSOLVE TO
DISSOLVE TO
DISSOLVE TO
DISSOLVE TO
DISSOLVE TO

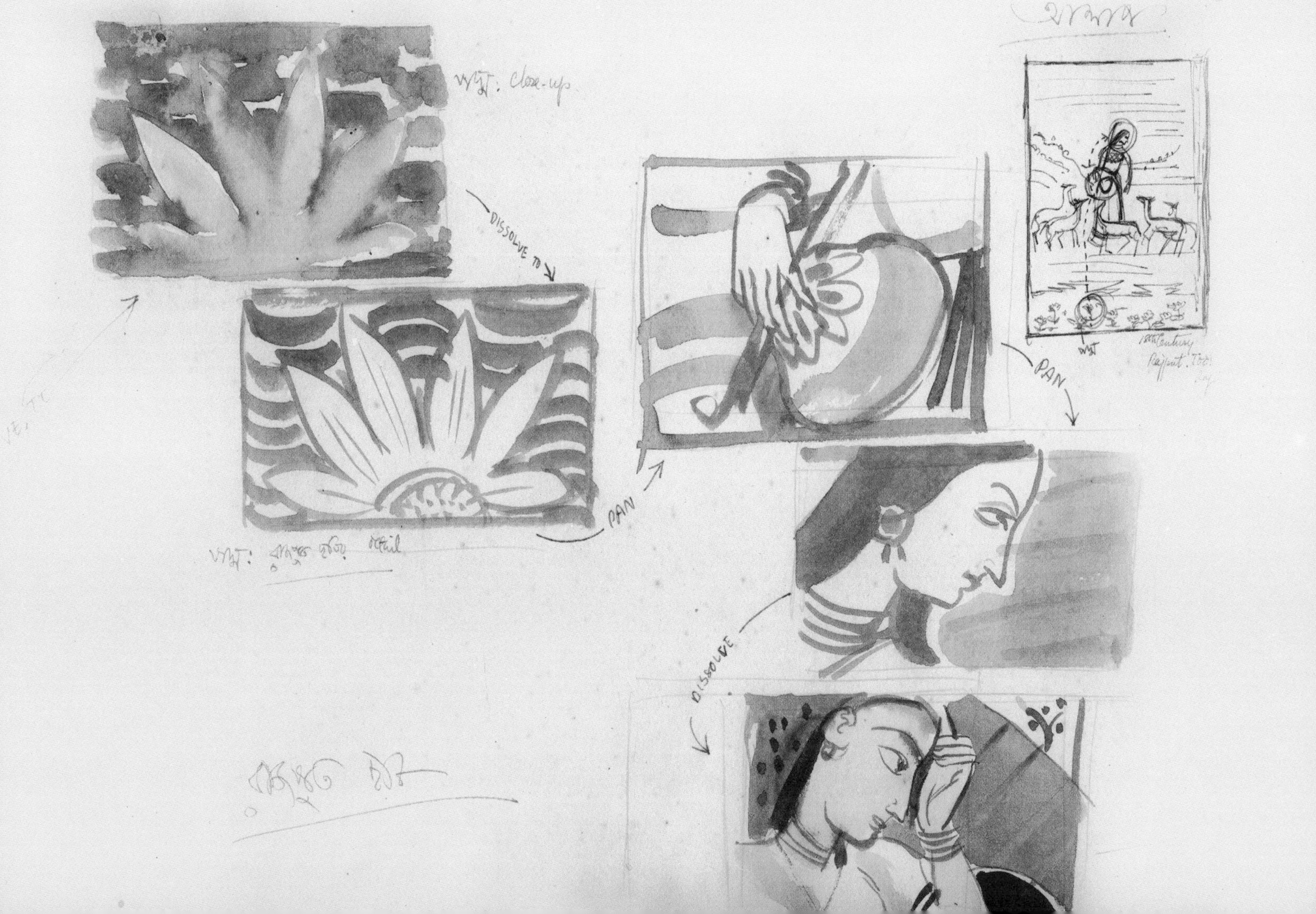
Close-up
DISSOLVE TO
PAN
PAN
DISSOLVE

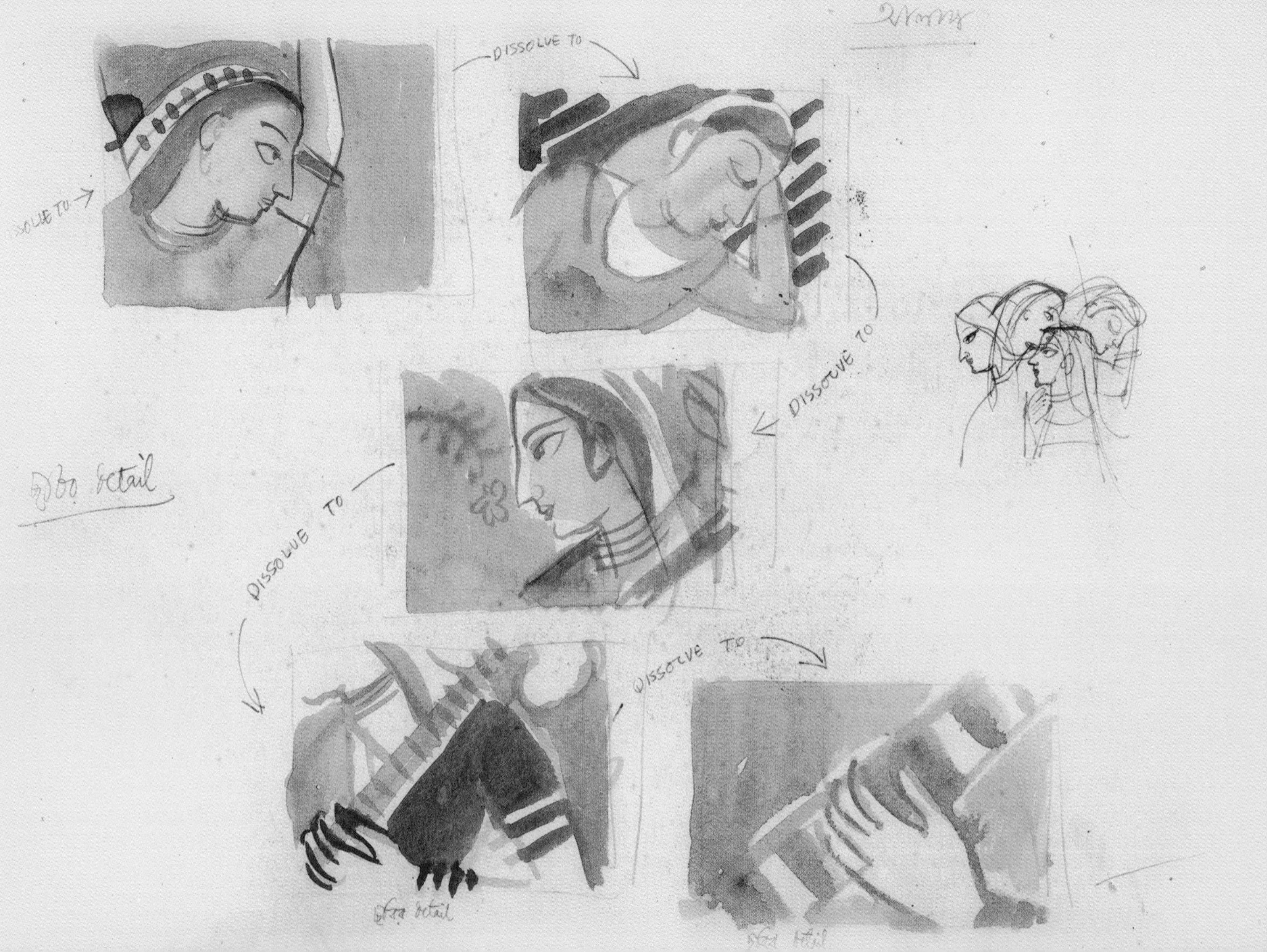
DISSOLVE TO
DISSOLVE TO
DISSOLVE TO
DISSOLVE TO
DISSOLVE TO
detail
detail
detail

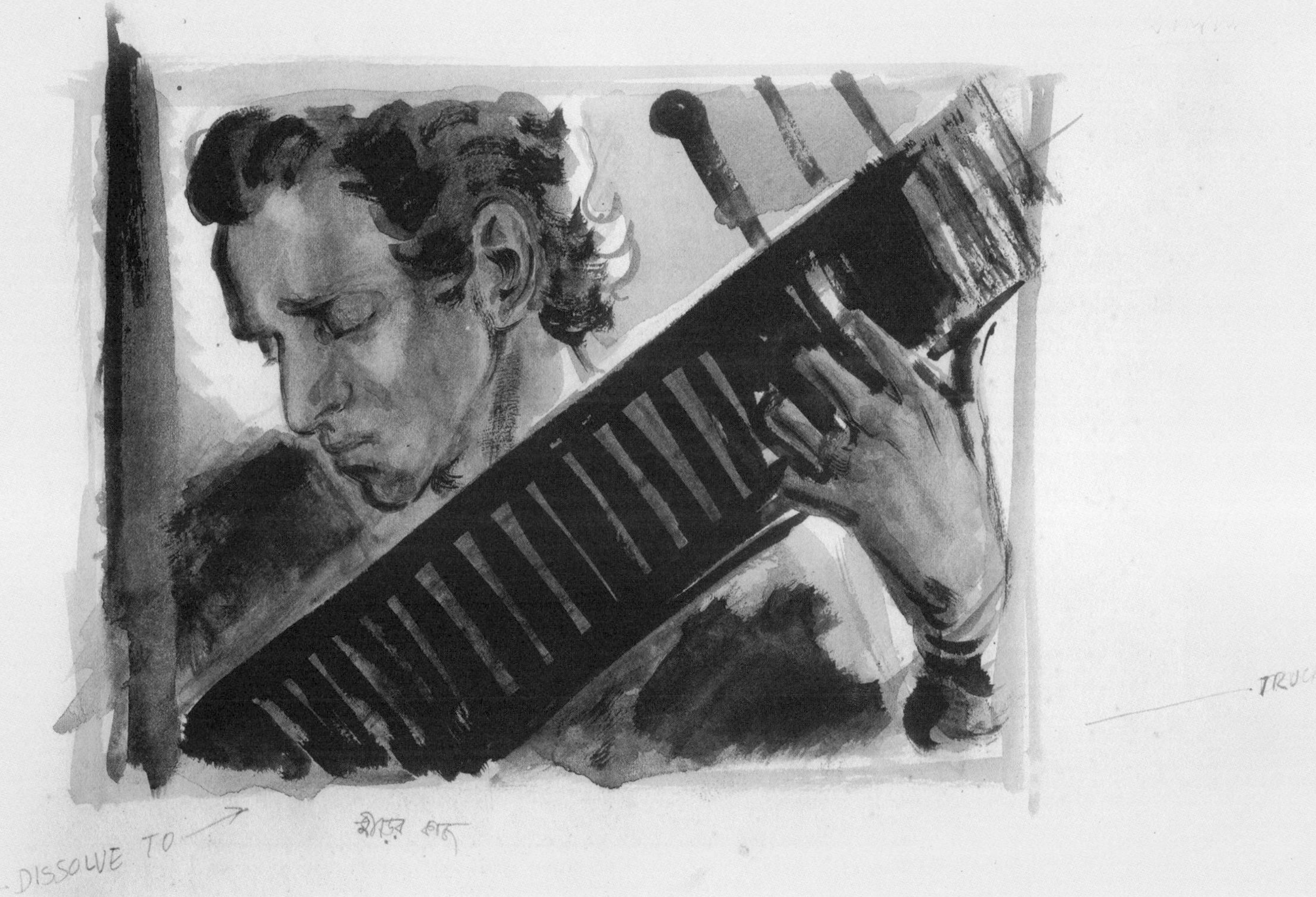
DISSOLVE TO
মীড়ের কাজ
TRUC

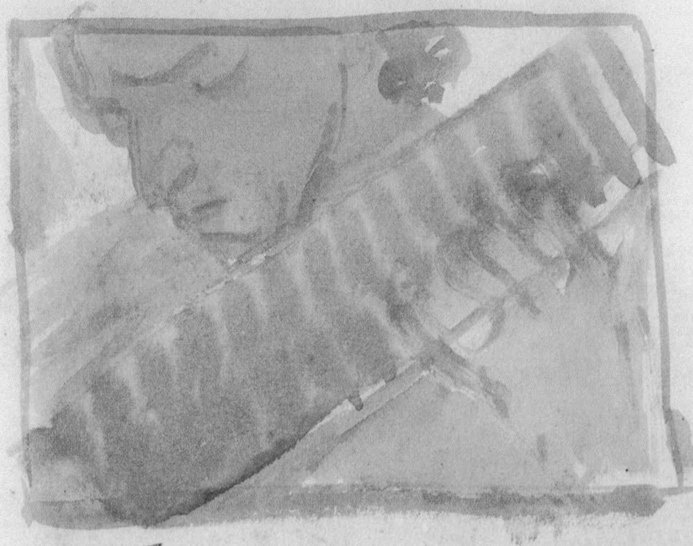

FORWARD

CUT

change of lighting

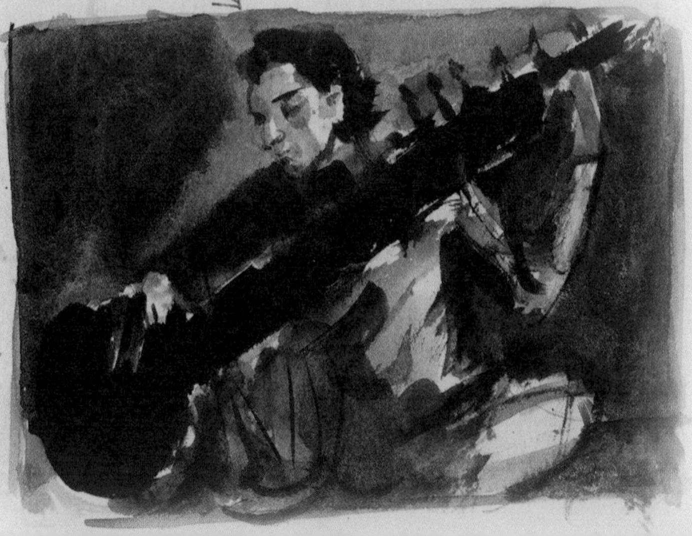

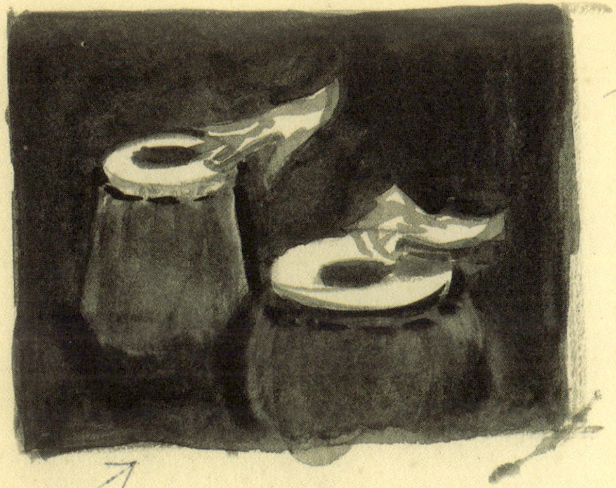

TRUCK BACK

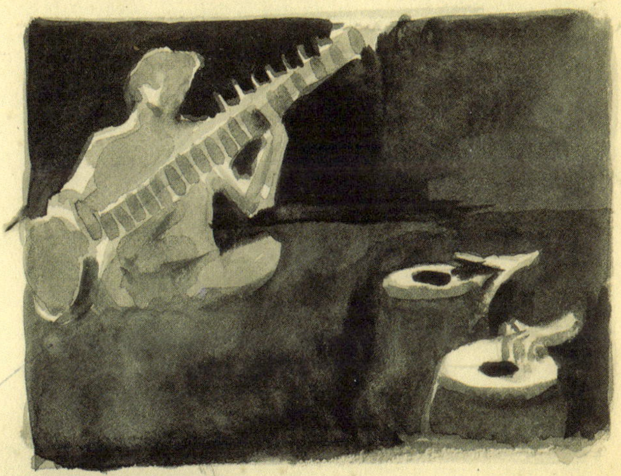

SWING TO

CUT

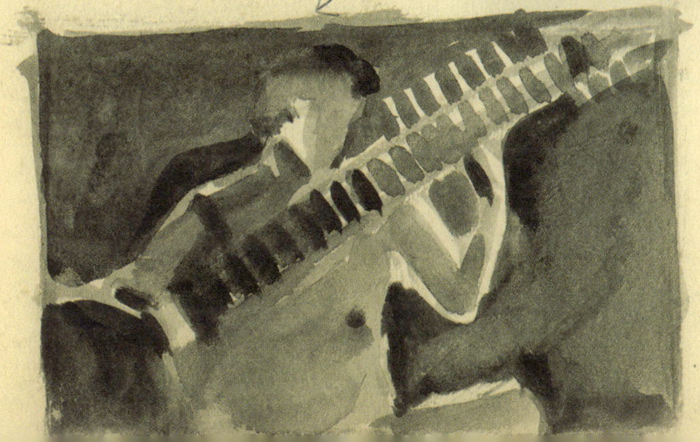

CUT

বিলম্বিত

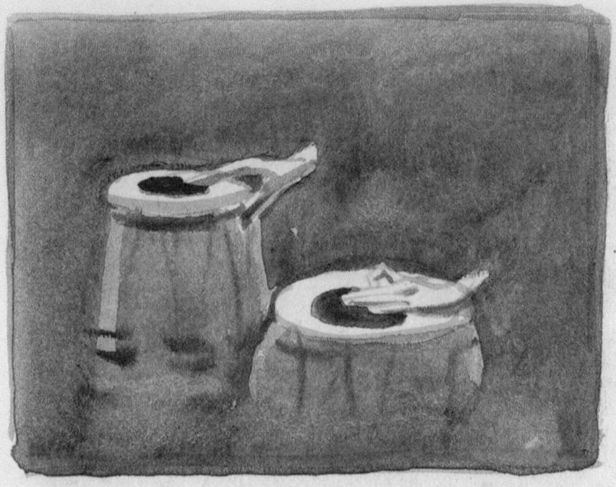

CUT →

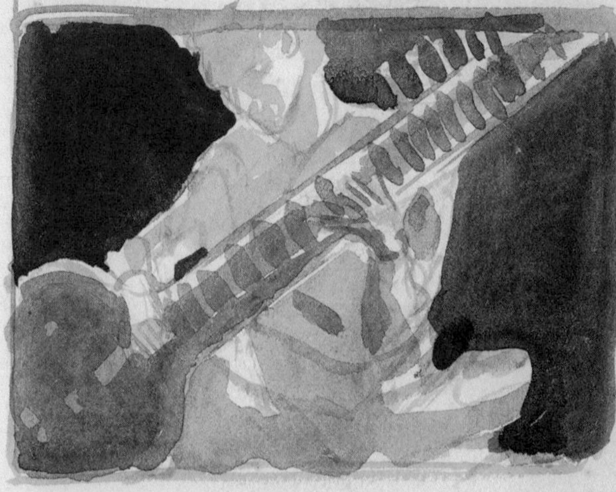

CUT

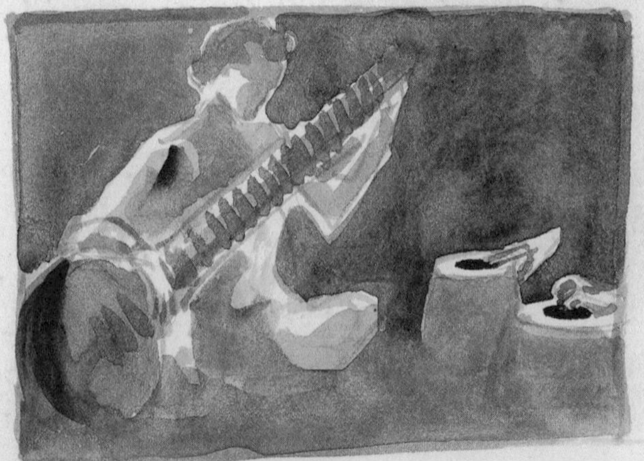

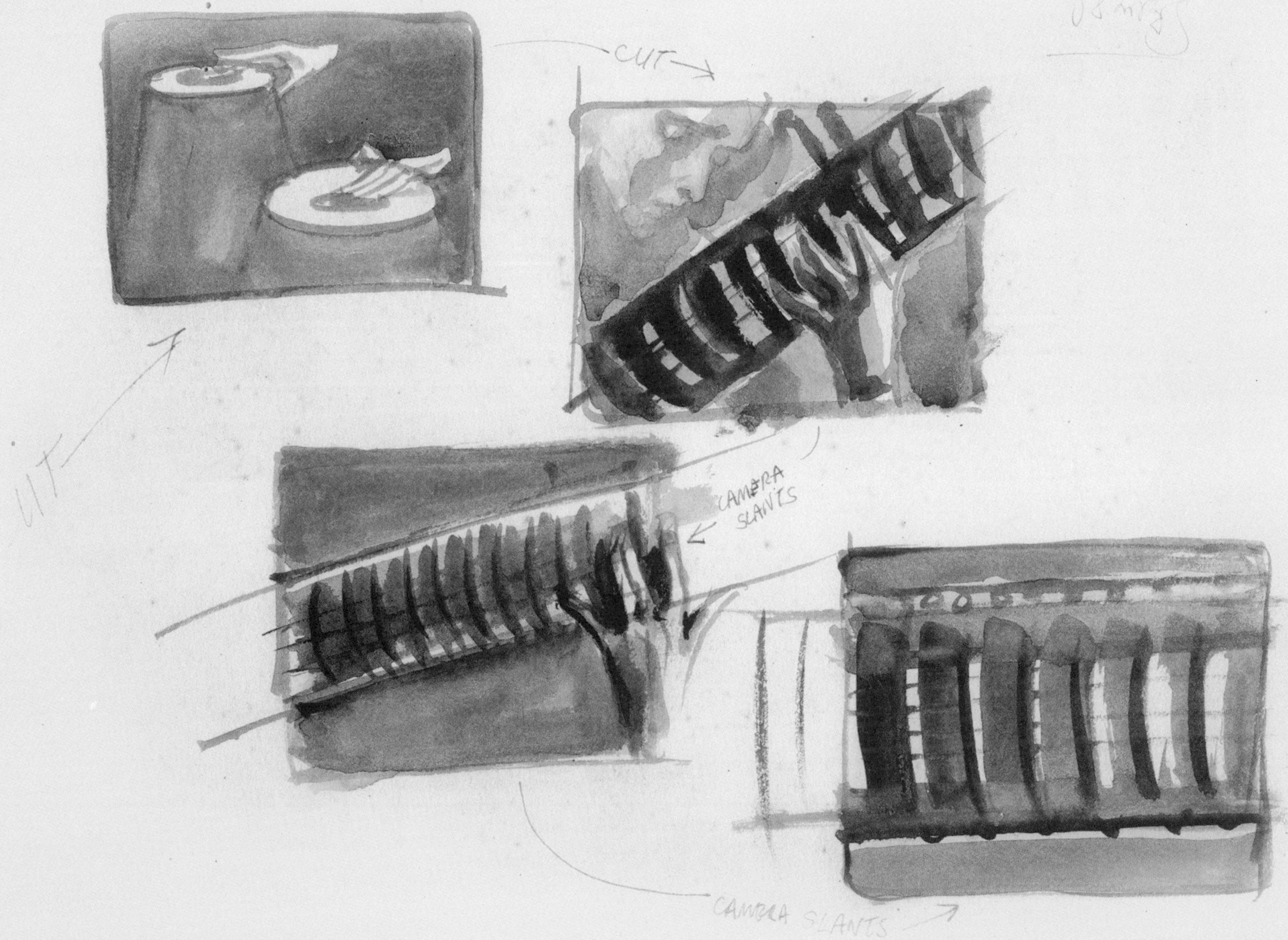
CUT
CUT
CAMERA SLANTS
CAMERA SLANTS

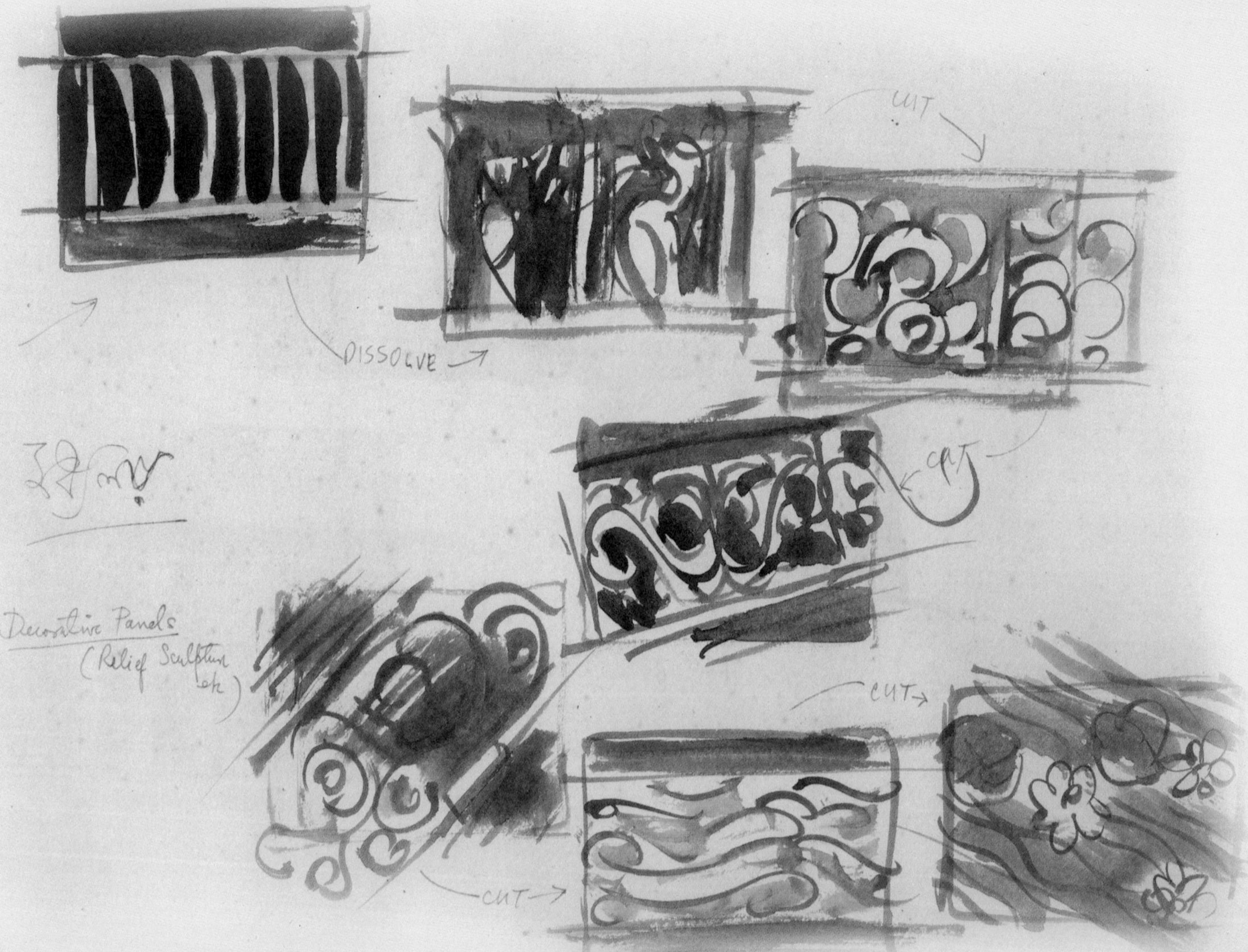

CUT
DISSOLVE
CUT
Decorative Panels
(Relief Sculpture etc)
CUT
CUT

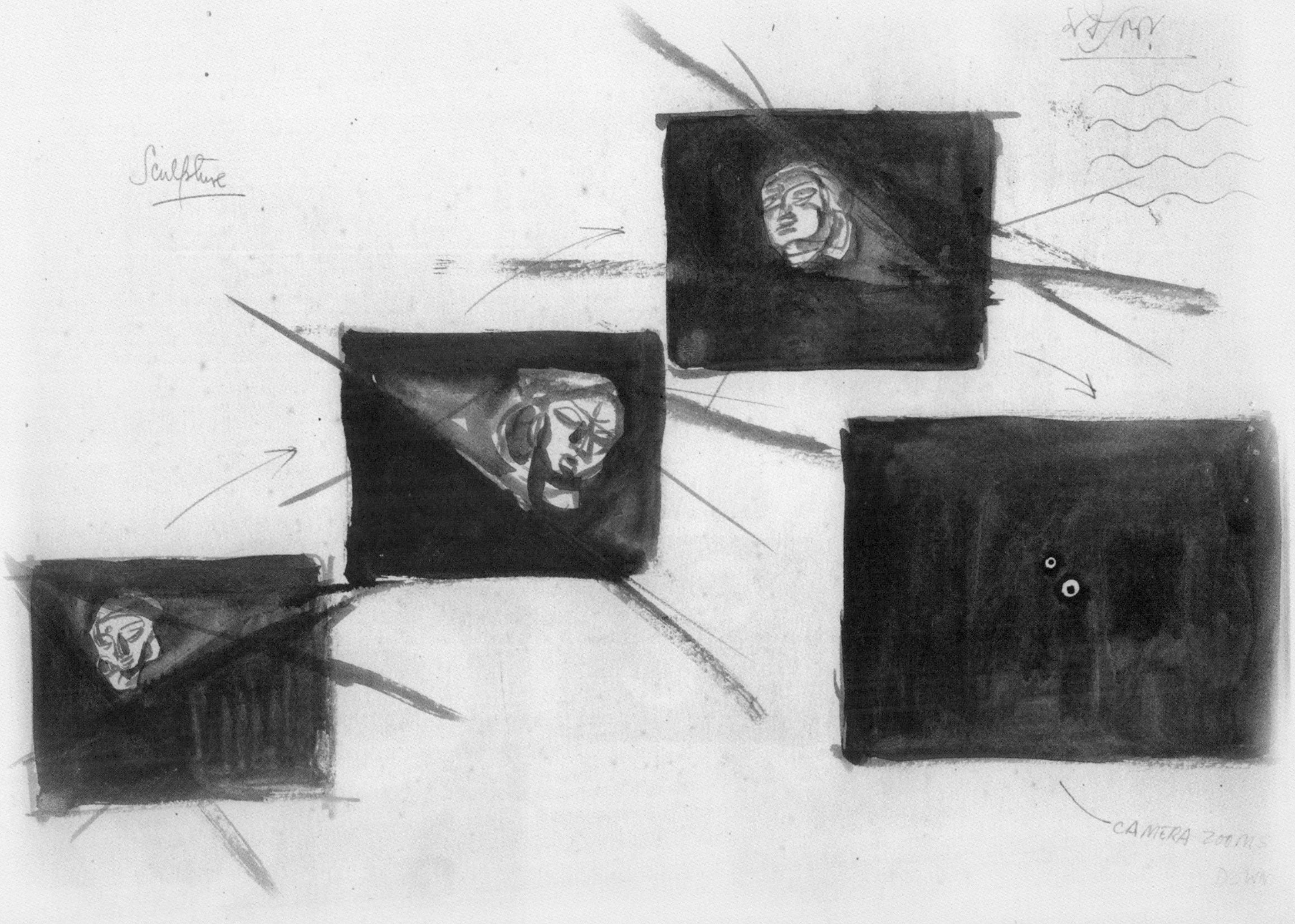
Sculpture
CAMERA ZOOMS

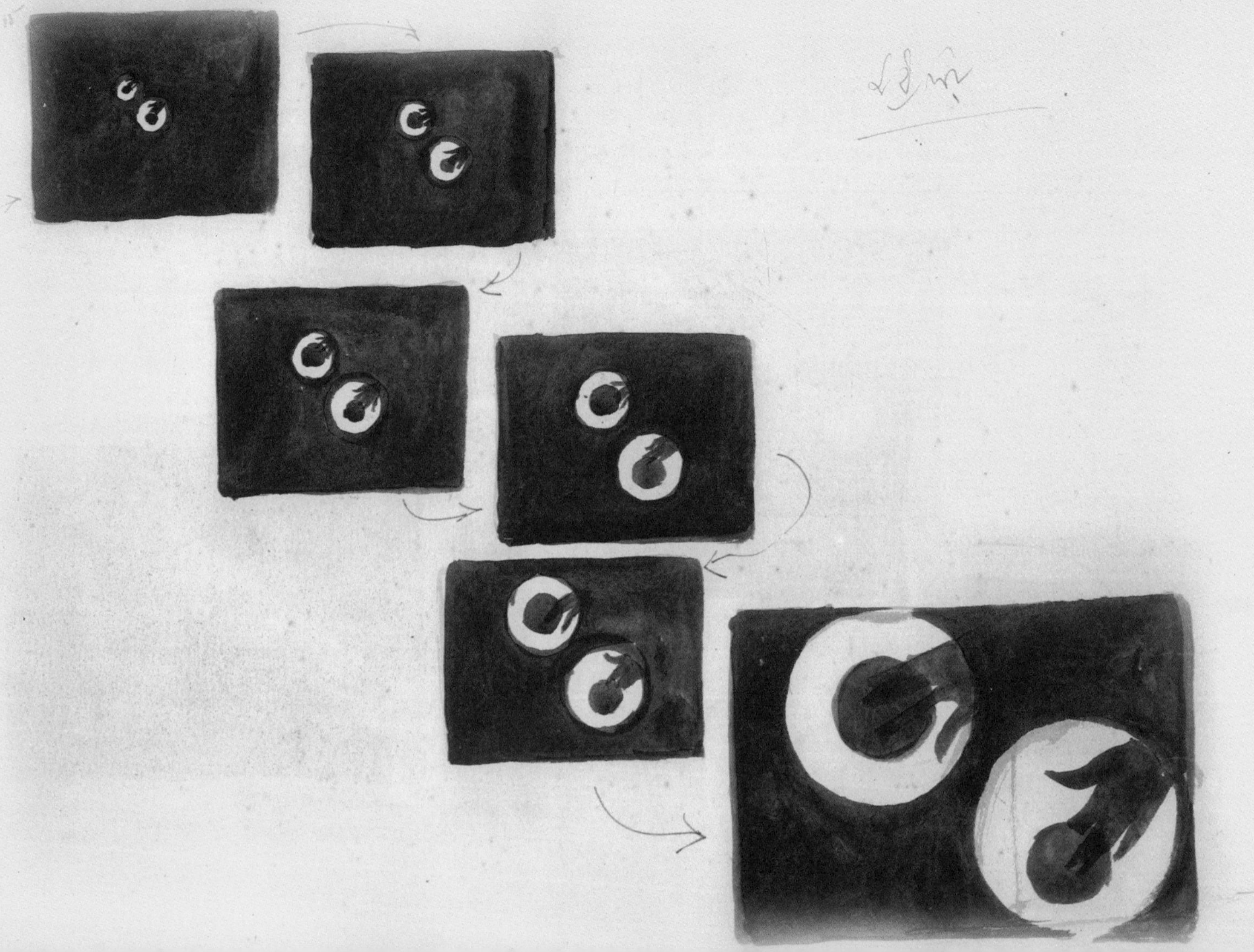

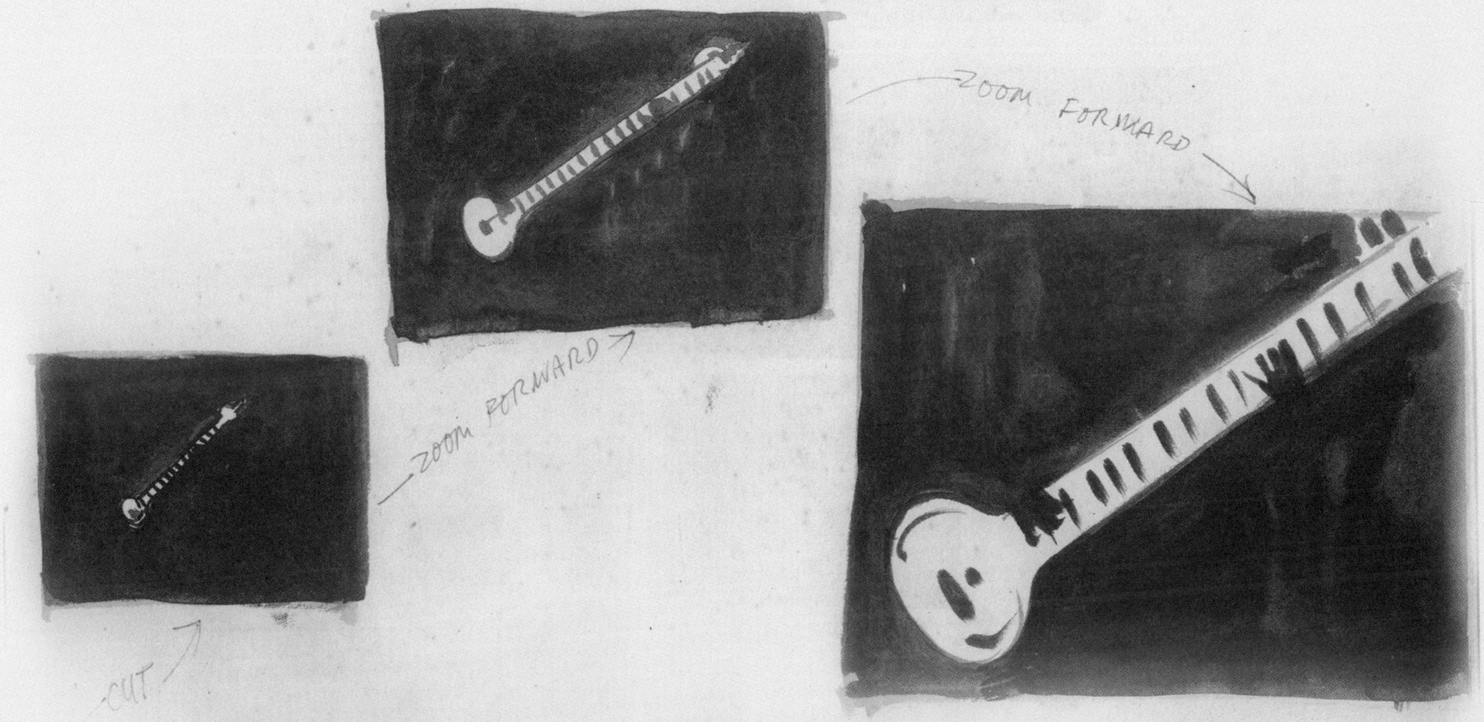

CUT
ZOOM FORWARD
ZOOM FORWARD

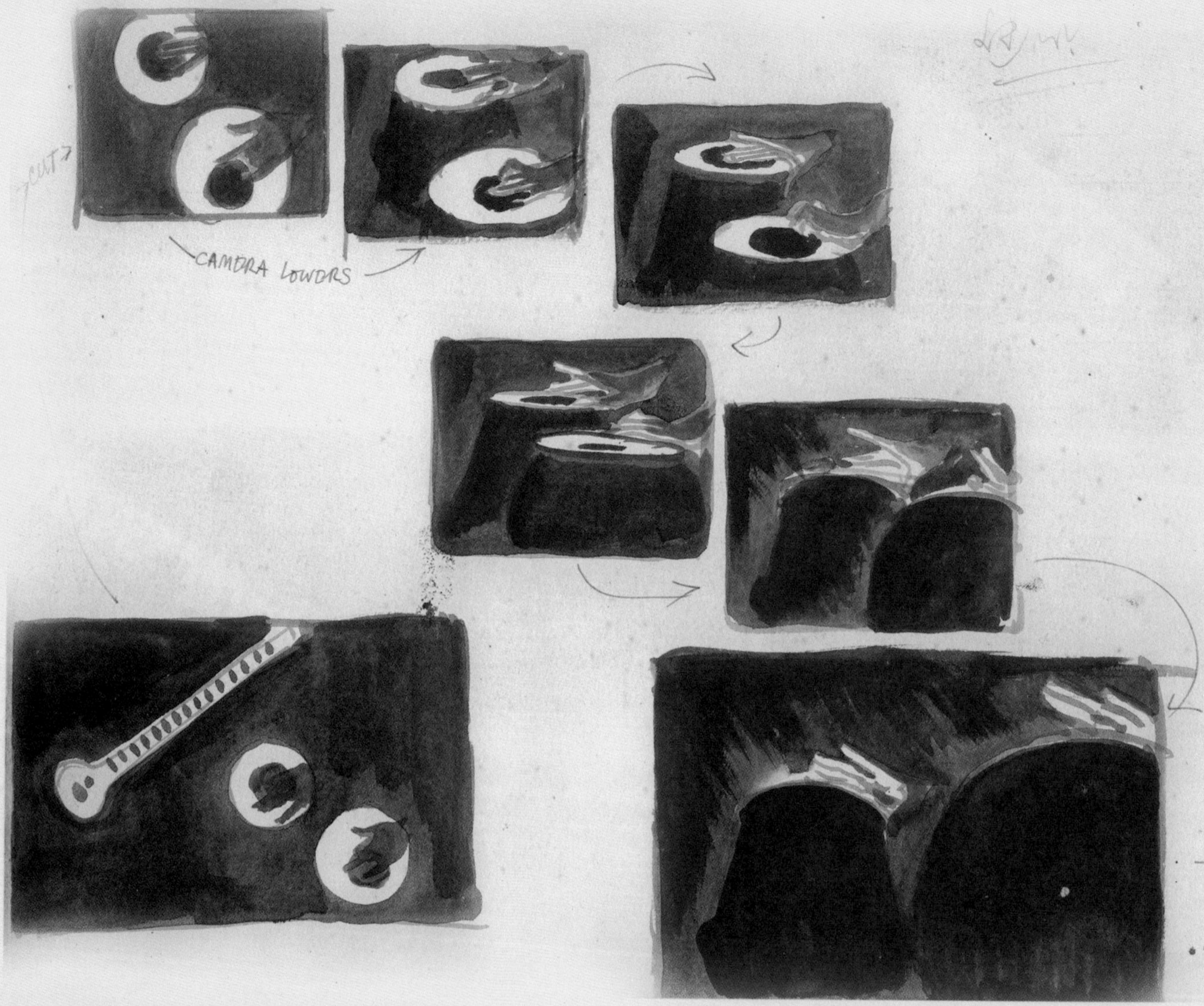
CUT
CAMERA LOWERS

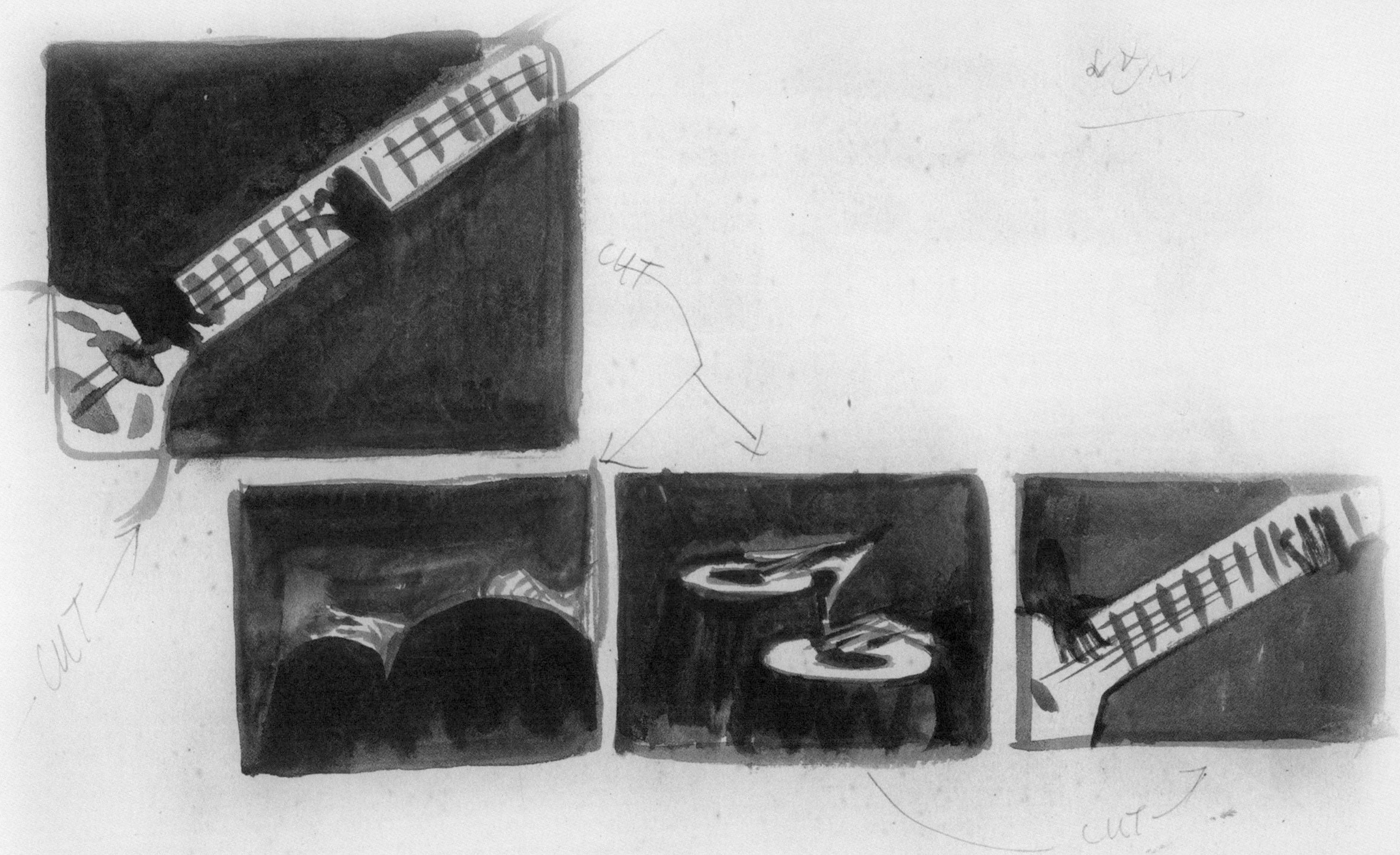
CUT
CUT
CUT

TILIS
DISSOLVE

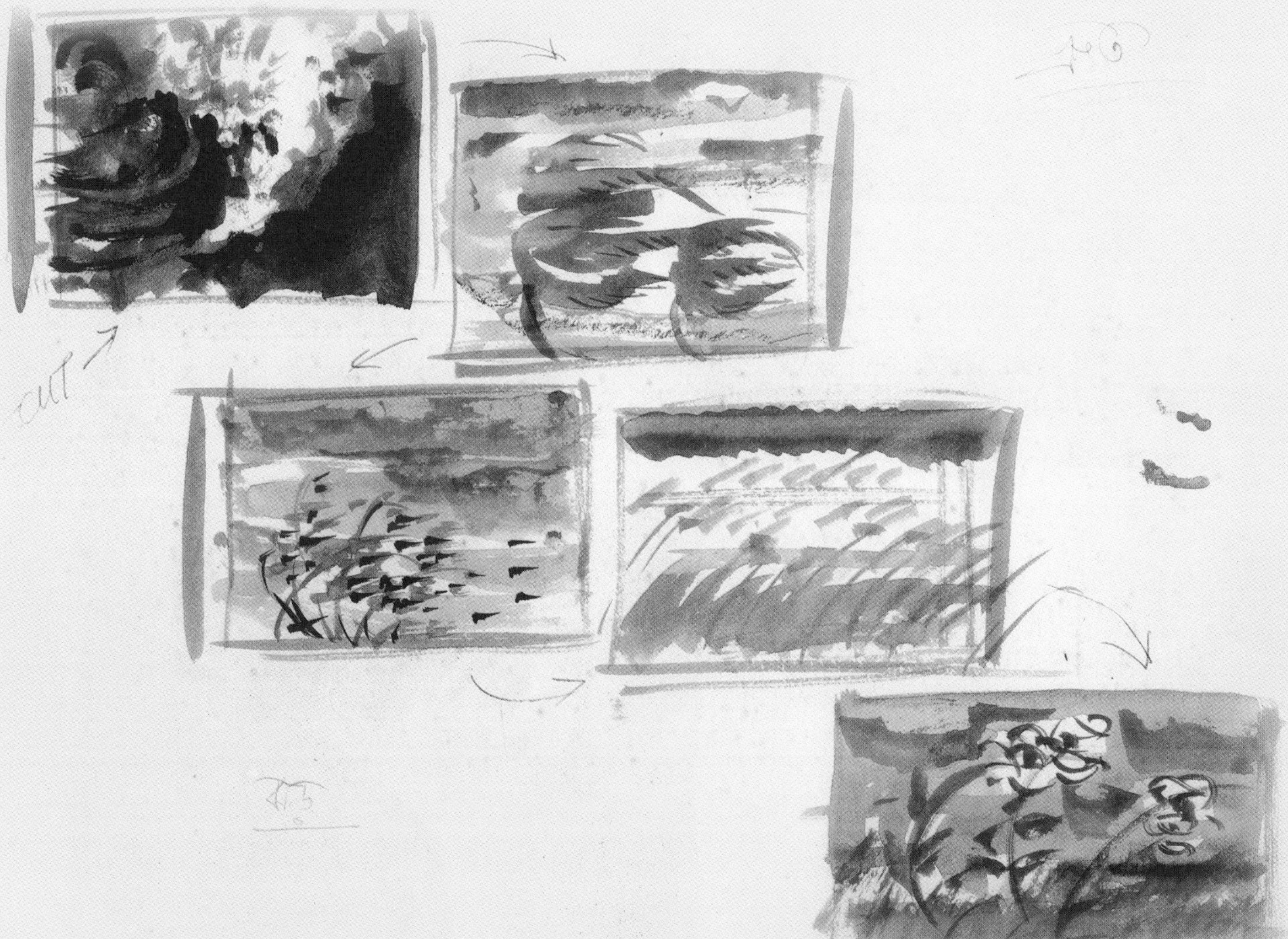
CUT

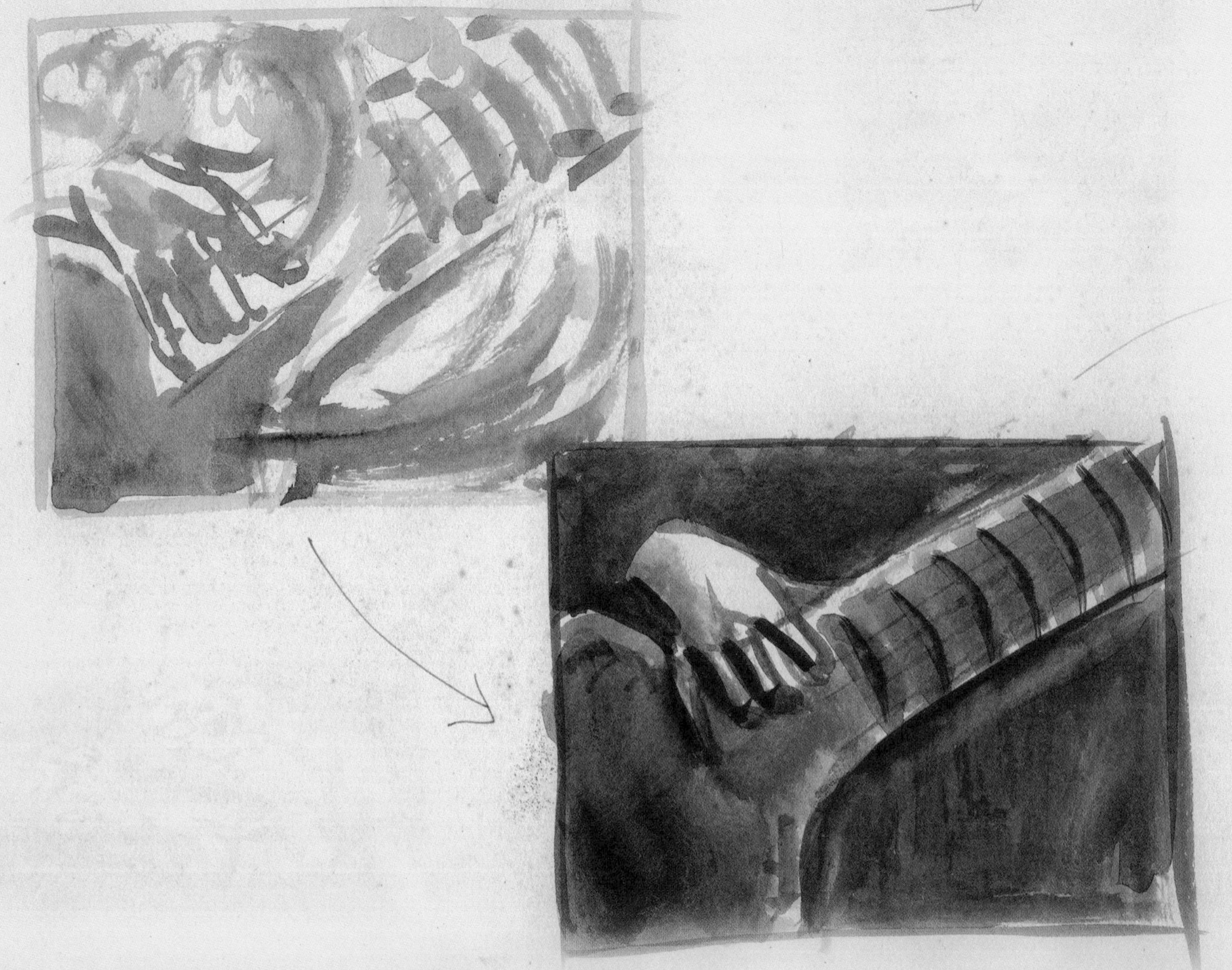

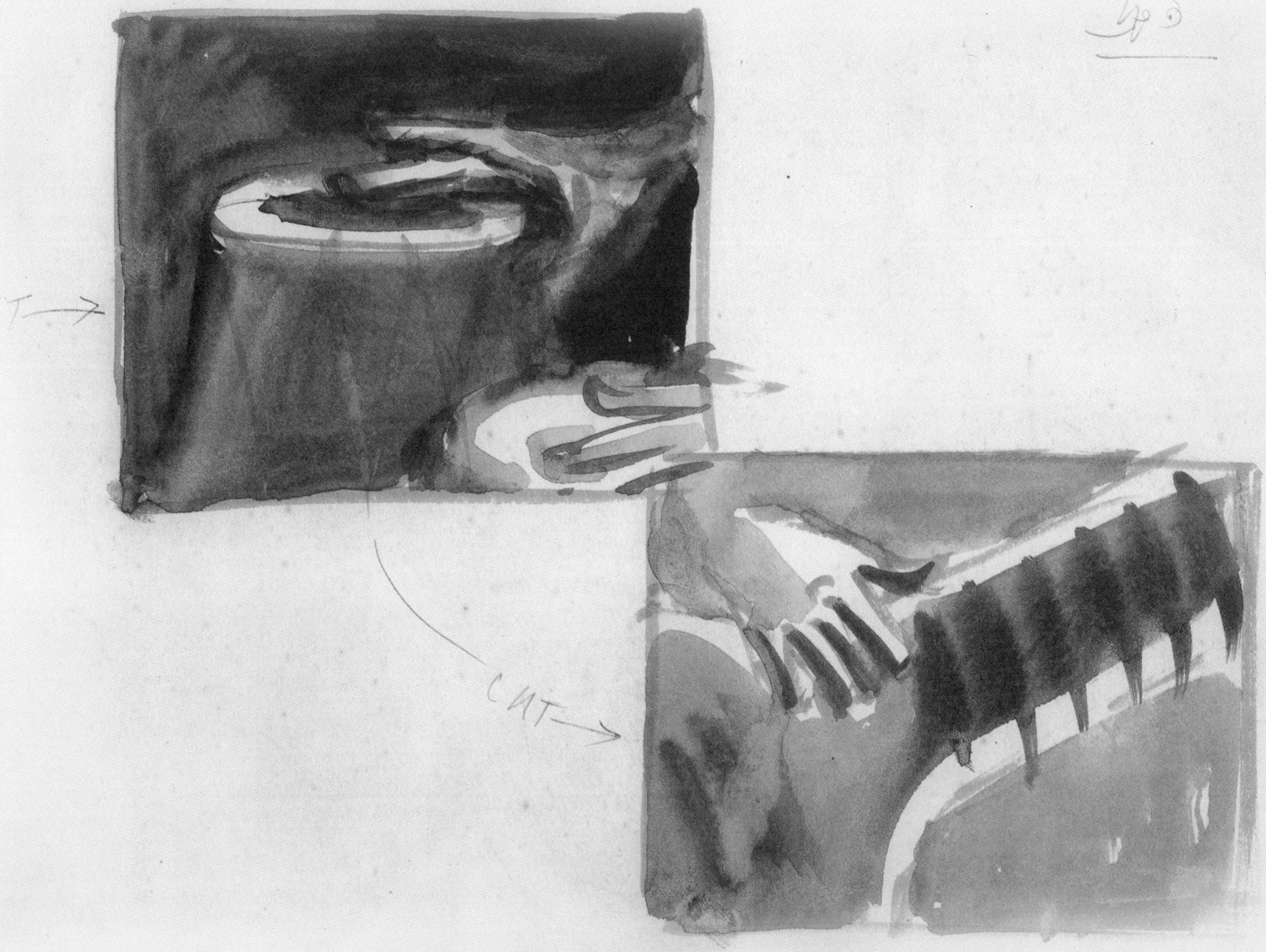
CUT

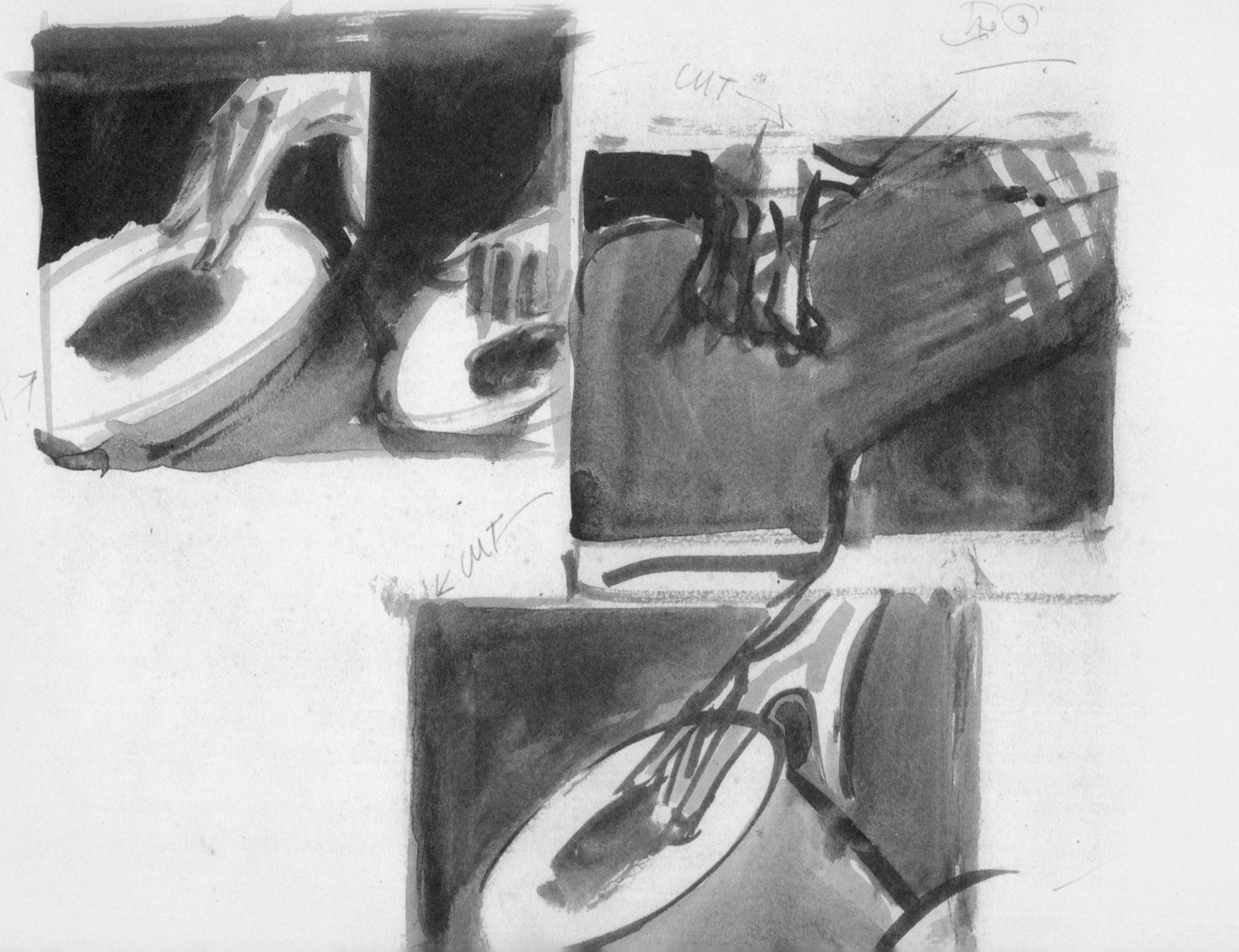
CUT
CUT

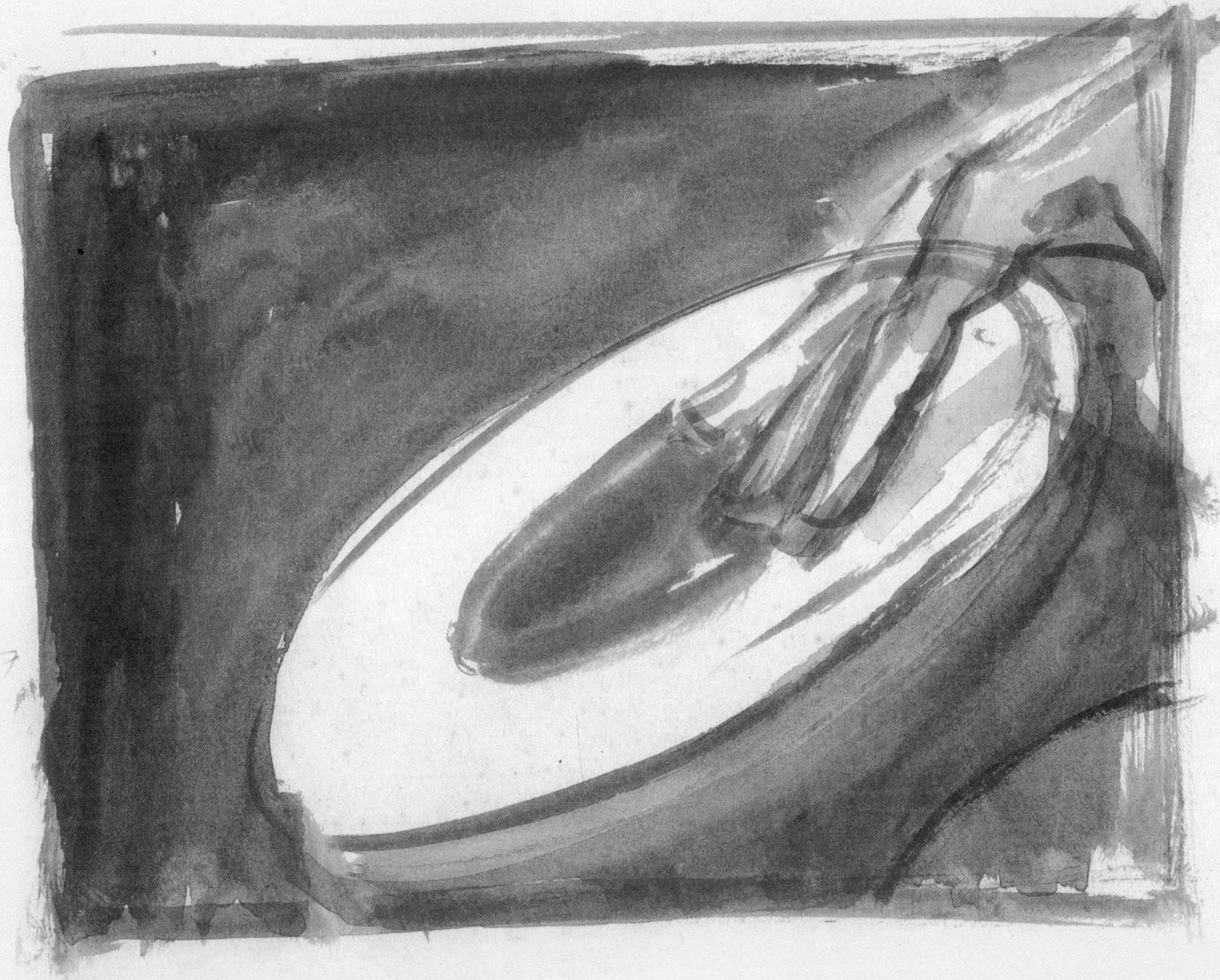

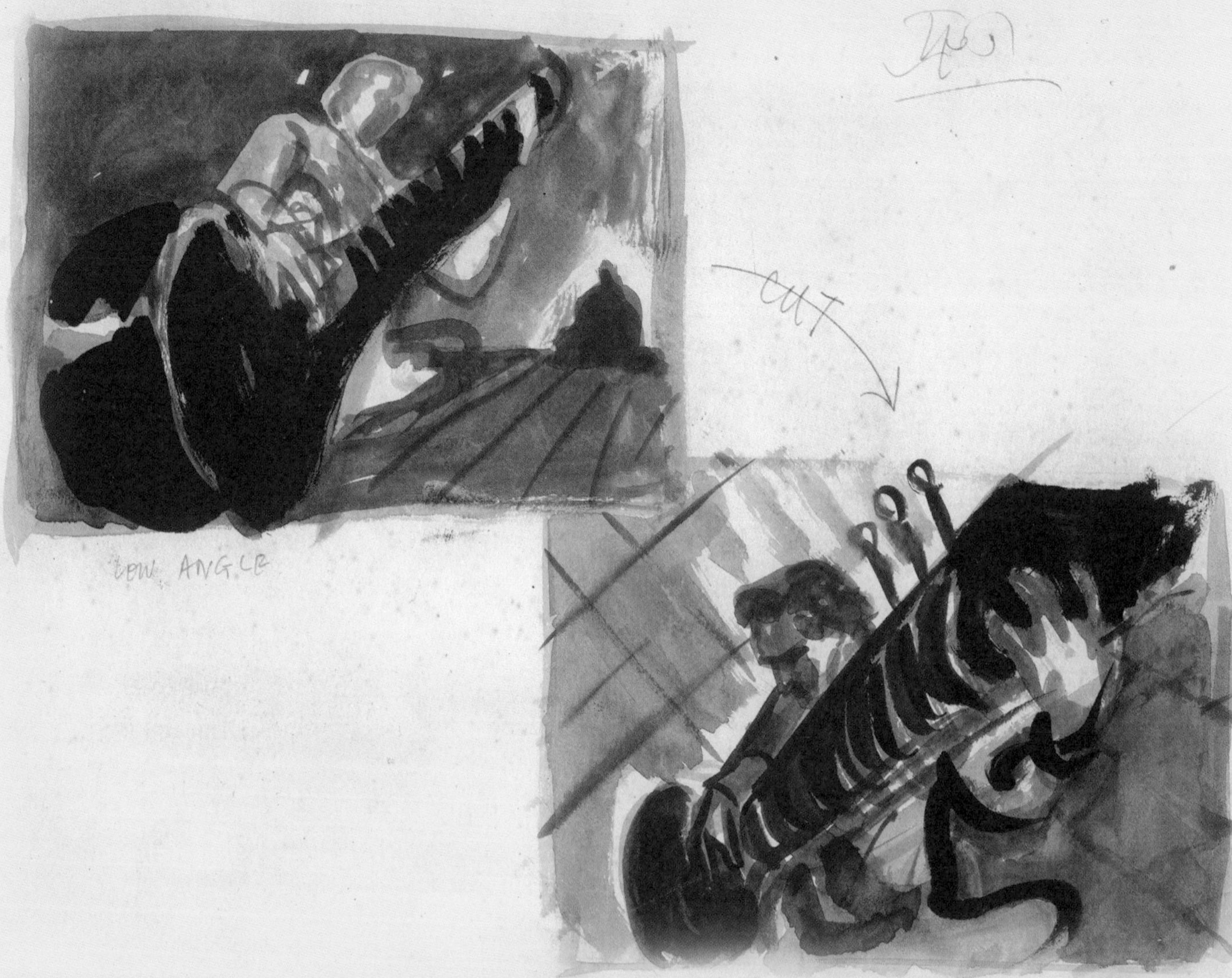
LOW ANGLE
CUT

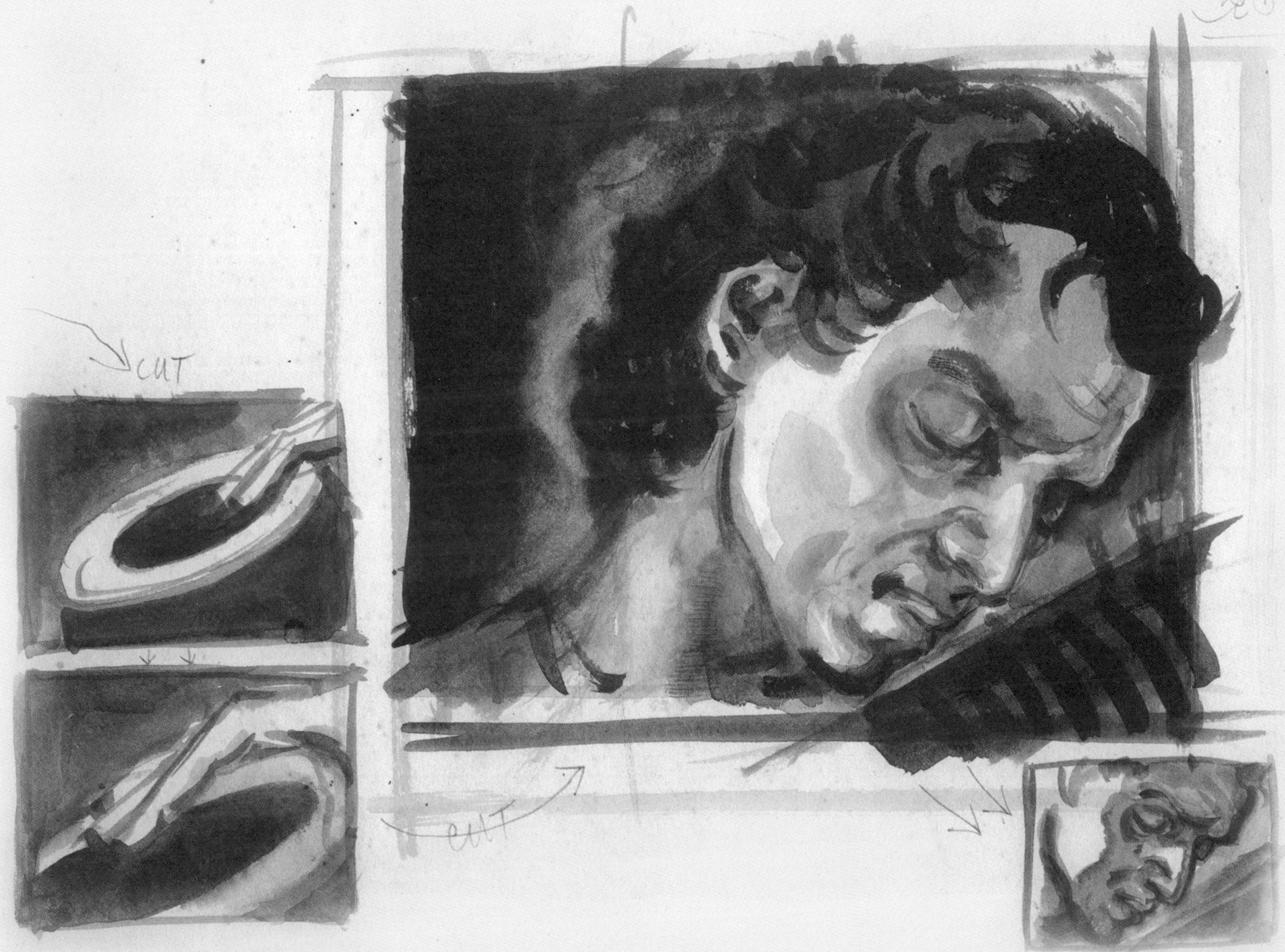
CUT
CUT

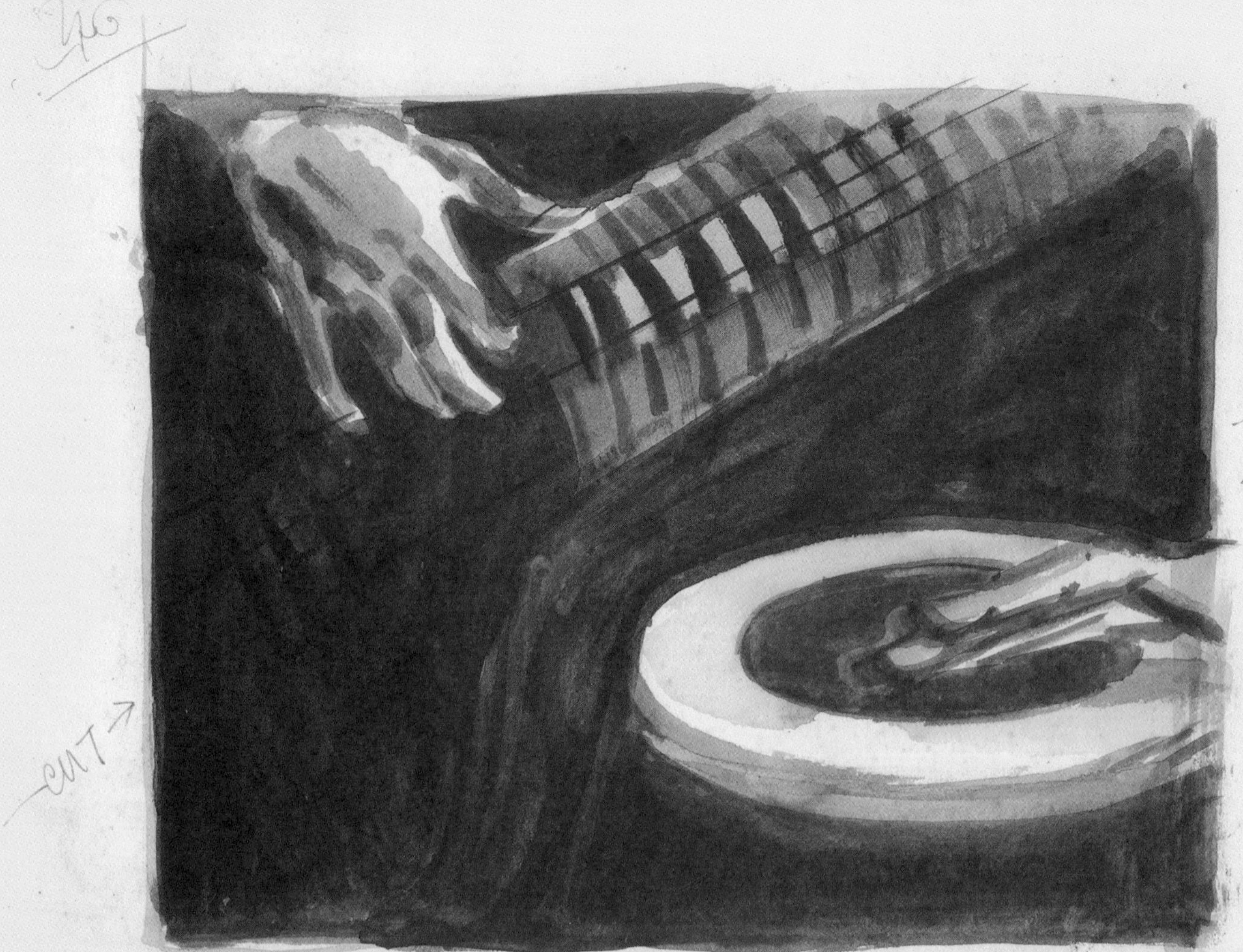
CUT

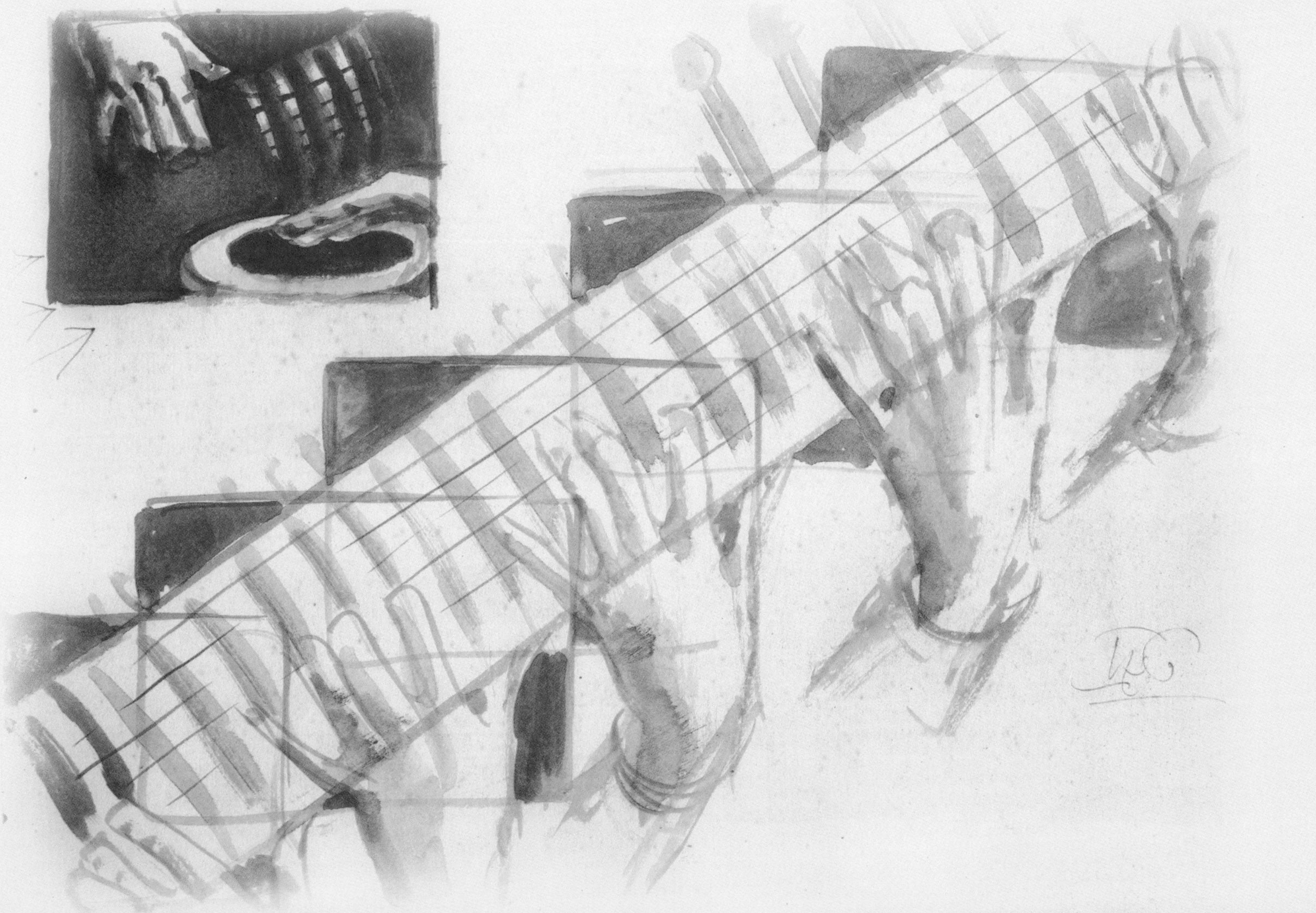

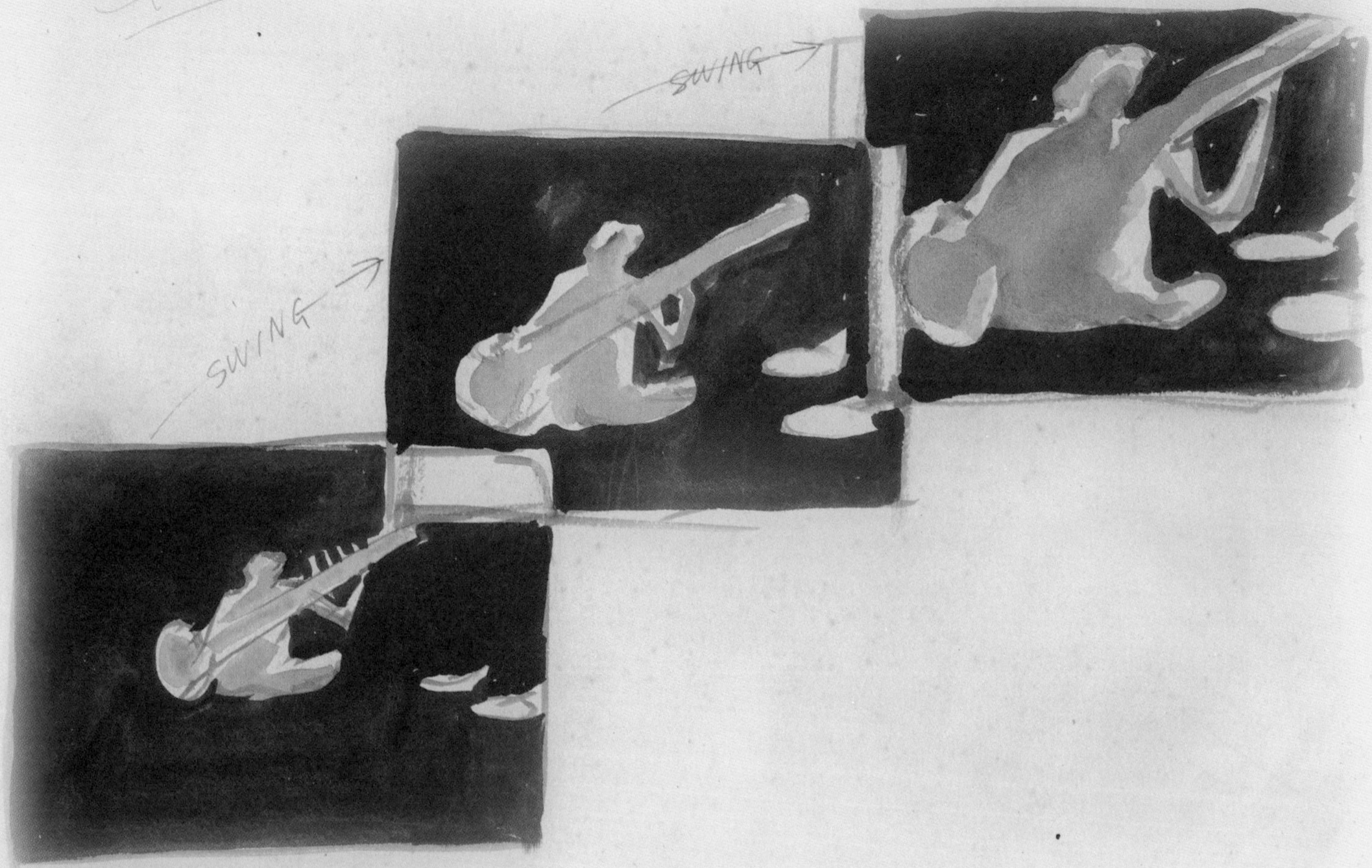
SWING
SWING

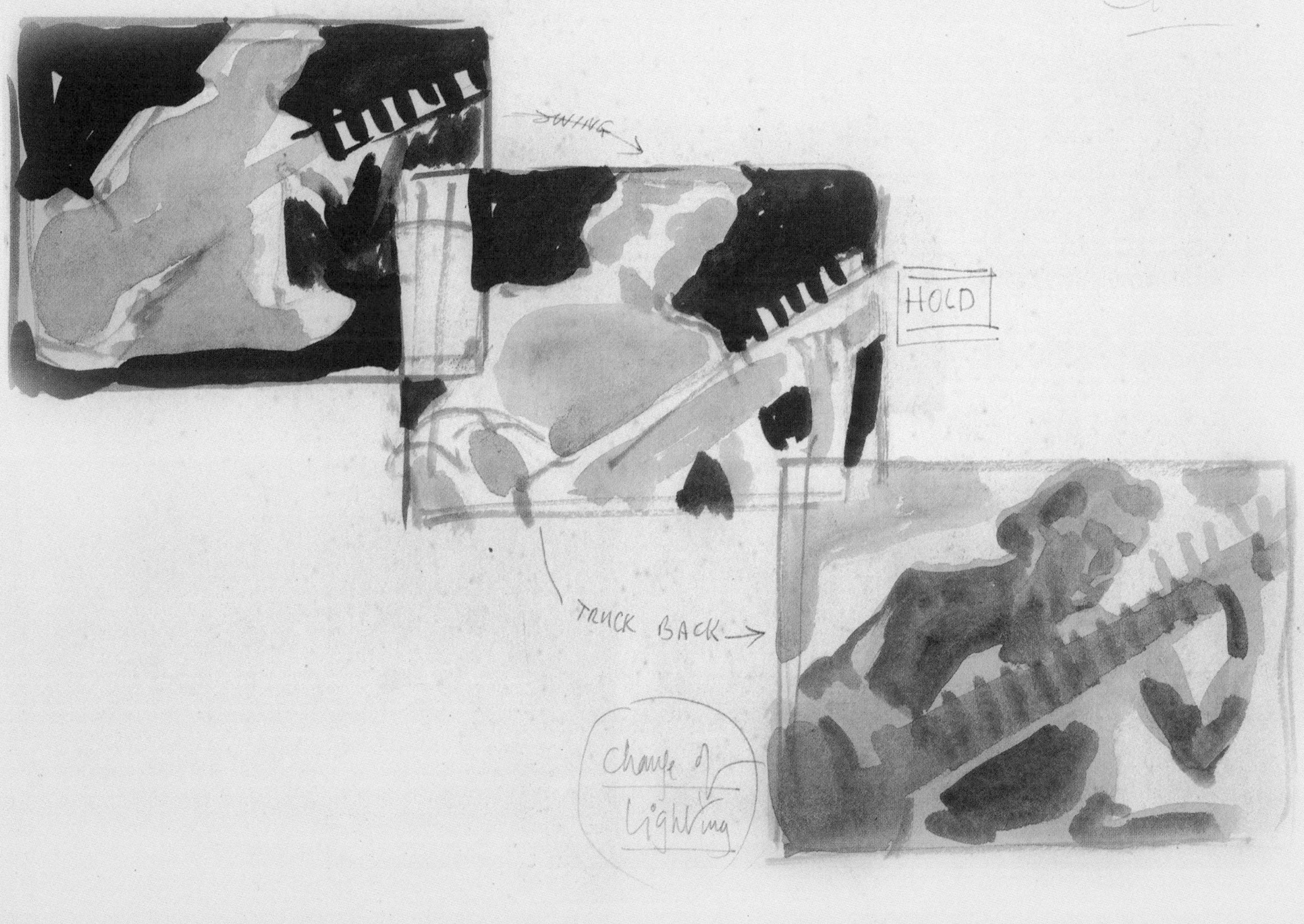
SWING
HOLD
TRUCK BACK
Change of Lighting

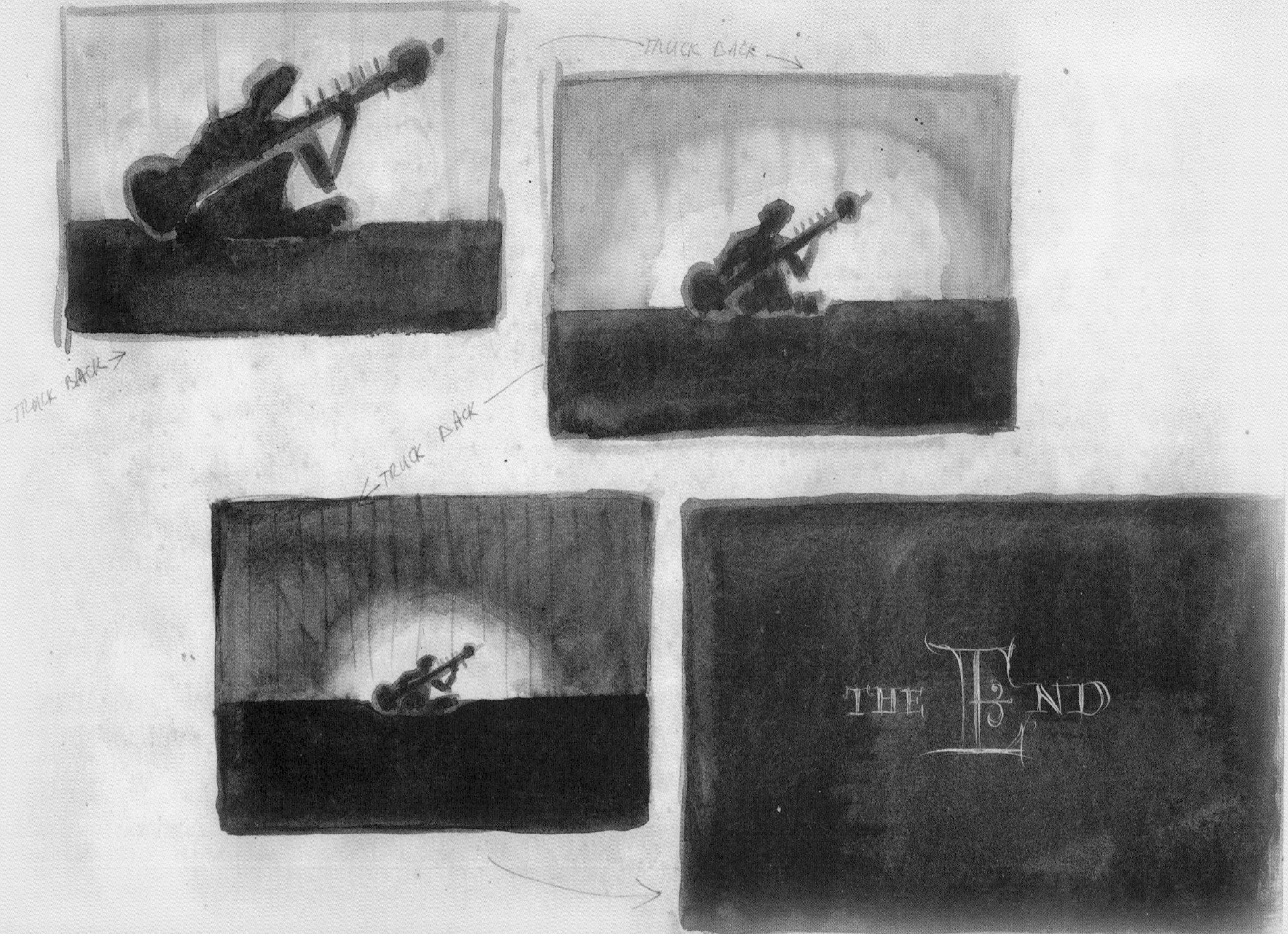
TRUCK BACK
TRUCK BACK
TRUCK BACK
THE END

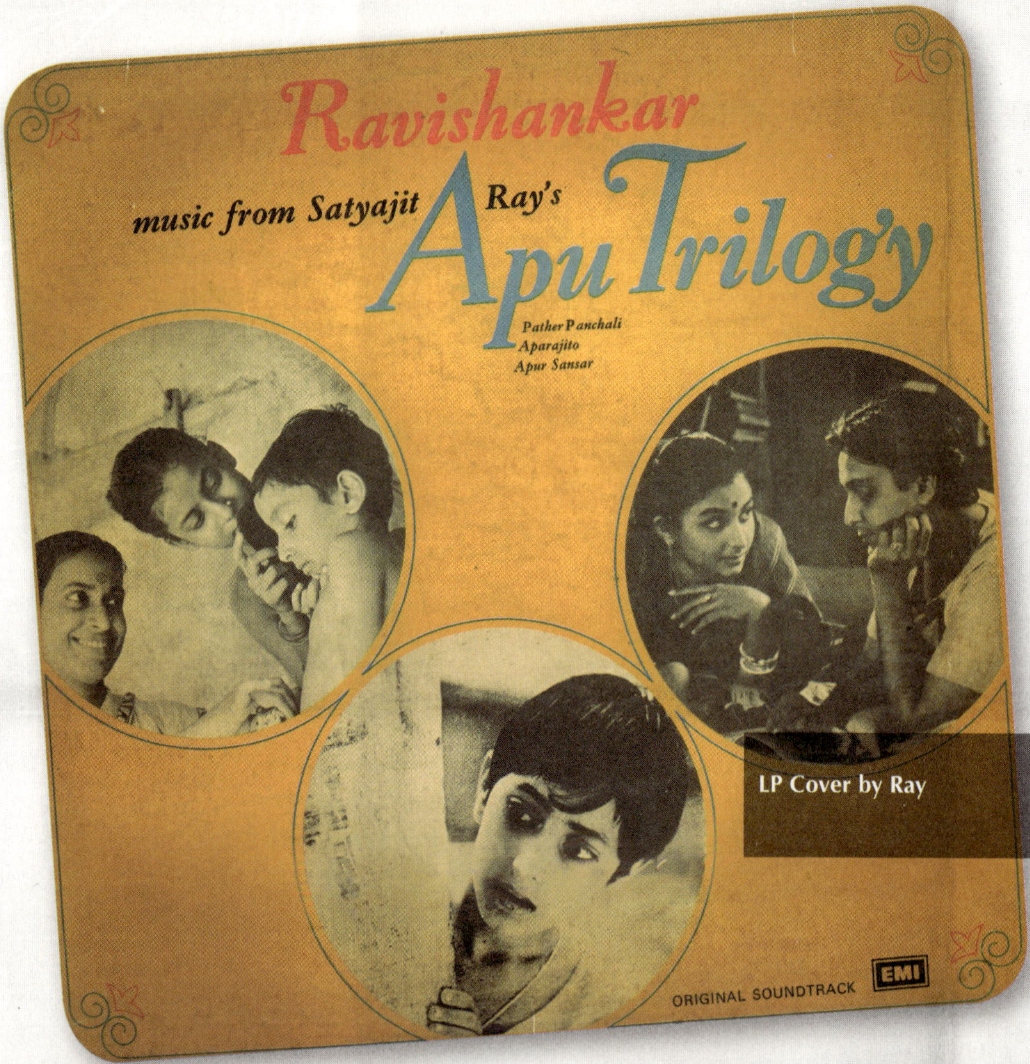

LP Cover by Ray

APU'S RENUNCIATION

SLEEVE NOTE FOR THE MUSIC OF SATYAJIT RAY'S APU TRILOGY EMI [INDIA], 1978, LP RECORDING

Satyajit Ray

Pather Panchali was still in production when I wrote to Ravi Shankar in Delhi asking him to compose the music for the film. I was an admirer of his music for the ballet *Discovery of India*, and was also familiar with some of the work he had done for films. Ravi Shankar agreed readily. However, when the time came to record the music, he was in the middle of a concert tour. There was no question of postponement, as we were forced with a release deadline, and certainly no question of replacing the composer. In the end, Ravi Shankar managed to come down for a day, was rushed to the projection room to be shown half of the film in a roughly edited version, and in the same afternoon composed and recorded the music in a single session ending in the small hours of the next morning.

One of the first things that Ravi Shankar did when I met him shortly after his arrival in Calcutta was to hum a line of melody which he said had occurred to him as a possible theme for the film. It was a simple tune with a wistful, pastoral quality which seemed to suit exactly the mood of the film. It went on to become the main motif of *Pather Panchali*.

Since I felt that in the short time that I had it would be too constricting for Ravi Shankar to have to compose to precise, predetermined footages, the method we used was to decide on the mood and instrumental combination of a particular scene, and then provide music well beyond the required length. In addition, we recorded about half-a-dozen three-minute pieces on the sitar in various ragas and tempos. This took care of the risk of running short at the time of fitting the music to the scenes in the cutting room. This is by no means an ideal method, but it has its advantages. For instance, the music that accompanies the ballet of the waterbugs in the film was originally played as one of the several variations on the main theme with no specific scene in mind. In fact, there was no scene of dancing insects in the film at this stage: it grew out of the music in the cutting room.

It was decided at the outset not to use any Western instruments in *Pather Panchali*. In addition to the sitar, we used the dilruba, the bhimraj (elder brother of the esraj), the sarod and the pakhawaj.

The same instruments, played solo and in various combinations, were used in *Aparajito*. Once again we had a hectic recording session, with Ravi Shankar humming, strumming, improvising and instructing at a feverish pace, and the indefatigable flautist-cum-assistant Aloke Dey transcribing the composer's ideas into Indian notation and dealing out the foolscap sheets to the tense handful who had to keep plucking and bowing and thumping with scarcely a breathing space.

In *Apur Sansar*, Ravi Shankar had to contend with a story that was much more varied in texture than the first two films of the trilogy. It begins in a squalid North Calcutta setting, shifts to the countryside for Apu's wedding, comes back to Calcutta and, after the death of Apu's wife, accompanies the disconsolate hero on his wanderings from seaside to sylvan woods, to the wild and hilly coalmining areas of Chhota Nagpur, returning finally to the Bengal countryside for the concluding scenes. Five Indian instruments were obviously inadequate to cope with all this, so Ravi Shankar decided to add violins and cellos (even the piano for one particular piece). Also, the usual hectic one-day session was abandoned, and the music was composed and recorded over three days.

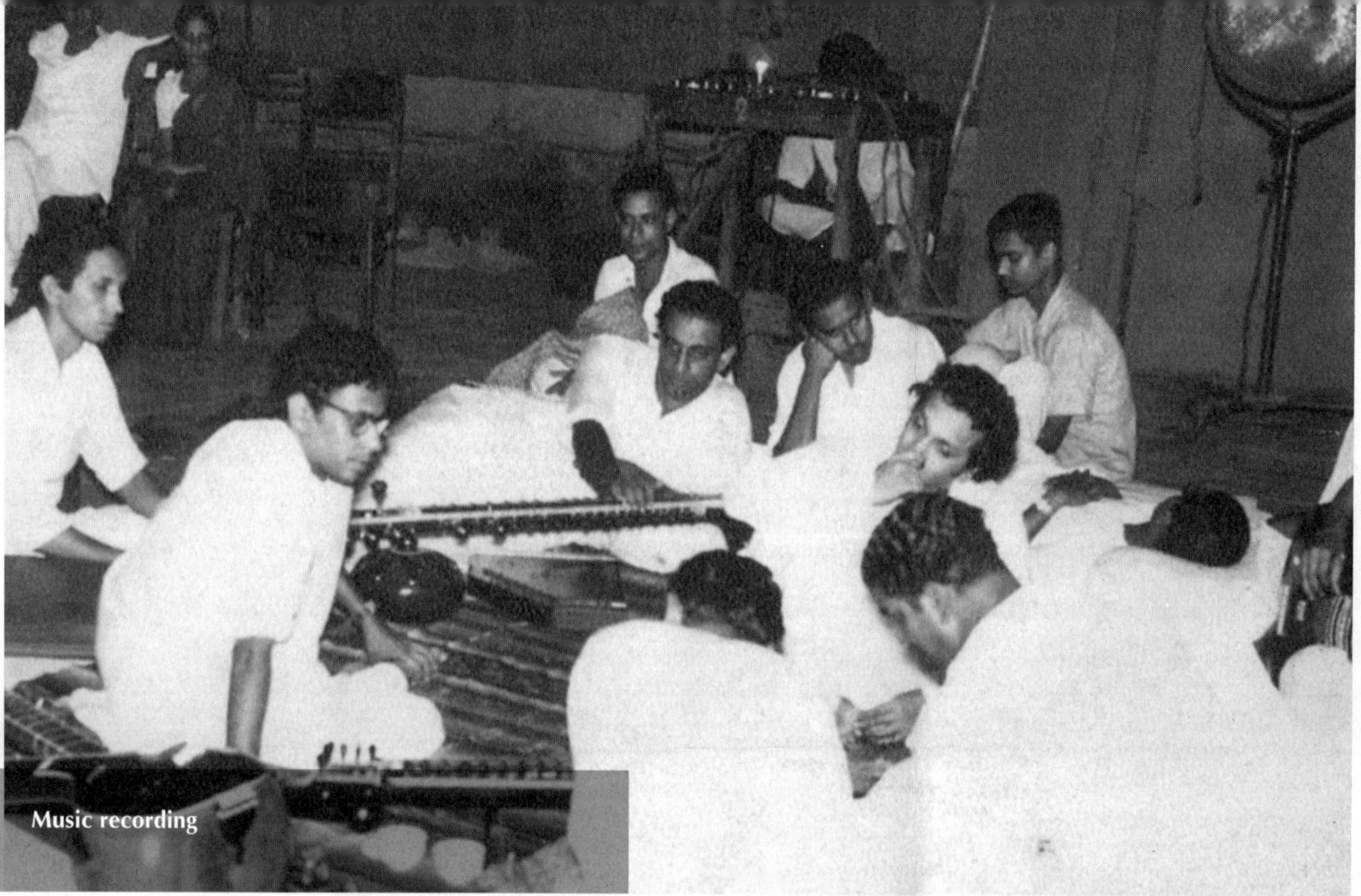

Music recording

MUSIC OF *PATHER PANCHALI*

EXTRACTS FROM *MY YEARS WITH APU: A MEMOIR*

Satyajit Ray

The shooting (of *Pather Panchali*) was now coming to a close and I had now to think of background music. I thought of Ravi Shankar partly because I knew him well personally and partly because I liked the sound of his instrument, the sitar, and hoped he would use it in his score.

Ravi Shankar then lived in Delhi. I wrote to him asking if he would agree to undertake the job. He willingly gave his consent. I had mentioned the time when I would need him and he said that there would be no problem.

Ravi Shankar arrived just for two days, one evening of which would be given over to a public recital. He had asked for only Indian instruments and we had got in touch with a flautist, Aloke Dey, who also provided musicians for a film score. Ravi Shankar was putting up with a musician friend of his and I went and saw him there.

The very first thing he told me was, 'I have a musical concept of your film.' He then proceeded to hum a tune. I was astonished. It was beautiful and just right for the film. He proceeded to discuss the method he would use for his work. I knew it would be unorthodox. Although Ravi Shankar had worked in a couple of films before and had composed some light music, I knew he would have to see the film before he could decide which portions called for music. He could then proceed to rehearse, taking into account the length of the passages and composing strictly within that given time. I knew this was not possible in this case for Ravi Shankar had kept only one day for me. He was essentially a virtuoso, to bind him down to a system he was not used to would be wrong. I didn't raise the question of method at all, but waited to see what he would do.

We arranged a screening the same afternoon. His recital was on the following day and whatever he was to do for the film had to be done today. Aloke Dey was asked to turn up with his musicians at the studio at 4 p.m. He himself was an excellent flautist and the other instruments to be used would consist of the sitar (which Ravi Shankar would play himself), a high-pitched instrument called the tar shehnai, a chamang (a string cymbal) and a percussion instrument called a cutachary. For one crucial scene I had a musical effect in my mind, which I decided to persuade Ravi Shankar to maintain. This was the scene in which Harihar returns from the city to discover from his wife that Durga had died.

Sarbajaya had remained silent the first few minutes and Harihar wrongly surmised that she was vexed because he had delayed his return. As Harihar hands her a sari he has bought for Durga, Sarbajaya can contain herself no longer and breaks out weeping. I had shot the scene as described and everything had worked out well except Sarbajaya's grief-stricken outburst. It didn't sound right. Then I saw it without sound and found that visually it was perfect and therefore decided to substitute the lamentation with a high controlled instrument like the tar shehnai, which would be suggestive of grief.

Ravi Shankar had time to see a little over half of the rough cut and greatly liked what he saw. Since he did not have the time to acquaint himself with the whole film and work out when music would be needed, I had to guide him using my instincts. There were about half a dozen highlights where music was obligatory and for the rest he could record several three-minute sitar pieces in various tempos and moods, which I could use as I thought fit at the time of final editing.

The recording of the music, which was actually improvised with notations hastily written down for the musicians, took eleven hours, starting at six and ending in the small hours of the next day. It was a marathon session and left us exhausted but happy, because most of the music sounded wonderful. The tar shehnai for the lament scene was played by one of its best exponents (D.M. Tagore), and I kept wishing that he stuck to the high notes of the raga Pat-Deep that was so aptly chosen by Ravi Shankar, for two full minutes.

In the short time that he had, Ravi Shankar could not provide the music for one of the more important scenes – that with the sweetmeat seller, as he goes peddling his sweets. I wanted music to keep time to his wobbling gait. This was devised later by my cameraman Subrata Mitra, who was also an excellent sitar player. That caused a problem for Ravi Shankar when he went on a tour of the States after *Pather Panchali* was released in 1958. At one of his recitals he was asked by a member of the audience to play the candy-man music from the film. Ravi Shankar had not seen the film yet, so he was not in a position to oblige, saying to the listener that he had forgotten how the music went.

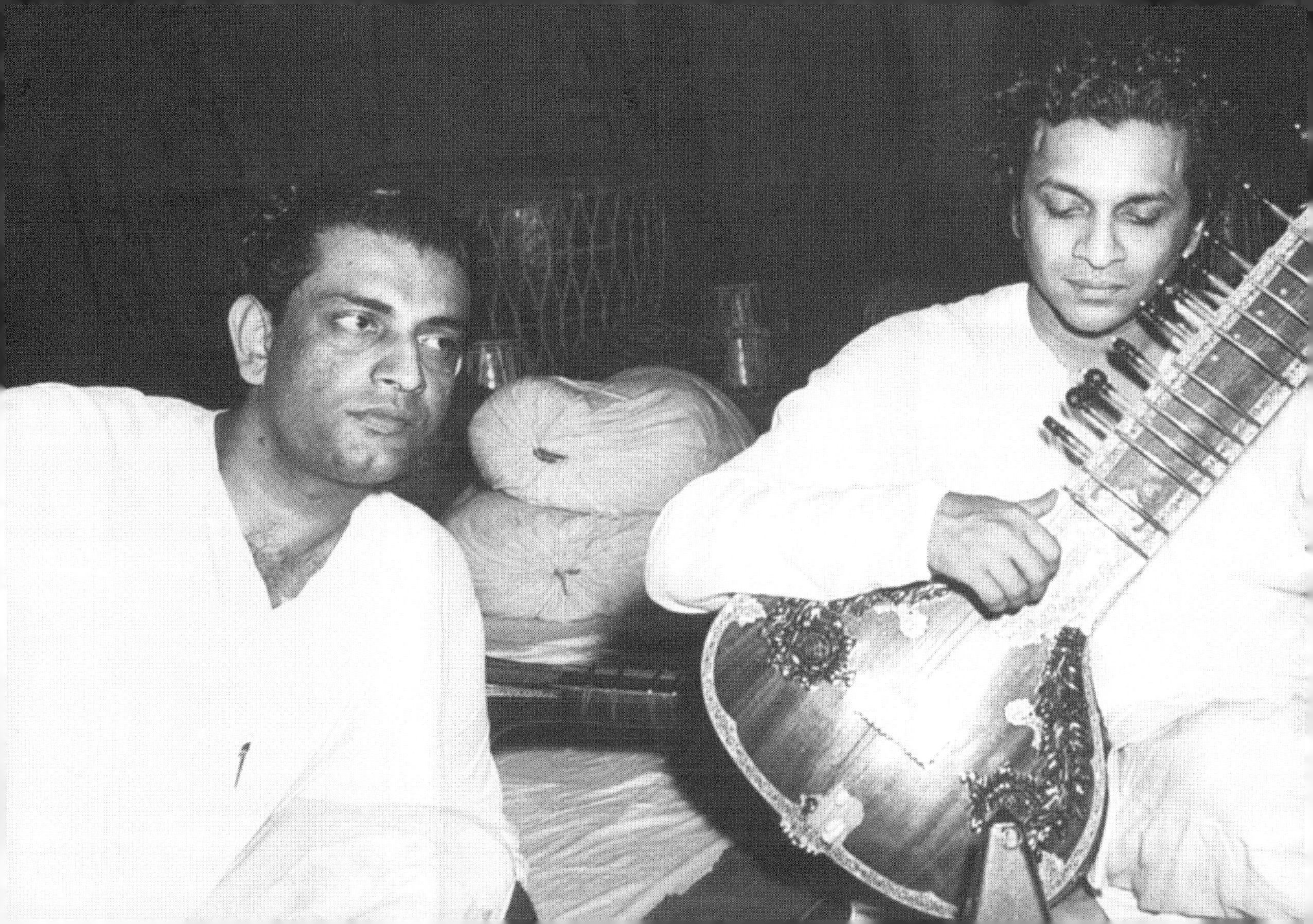

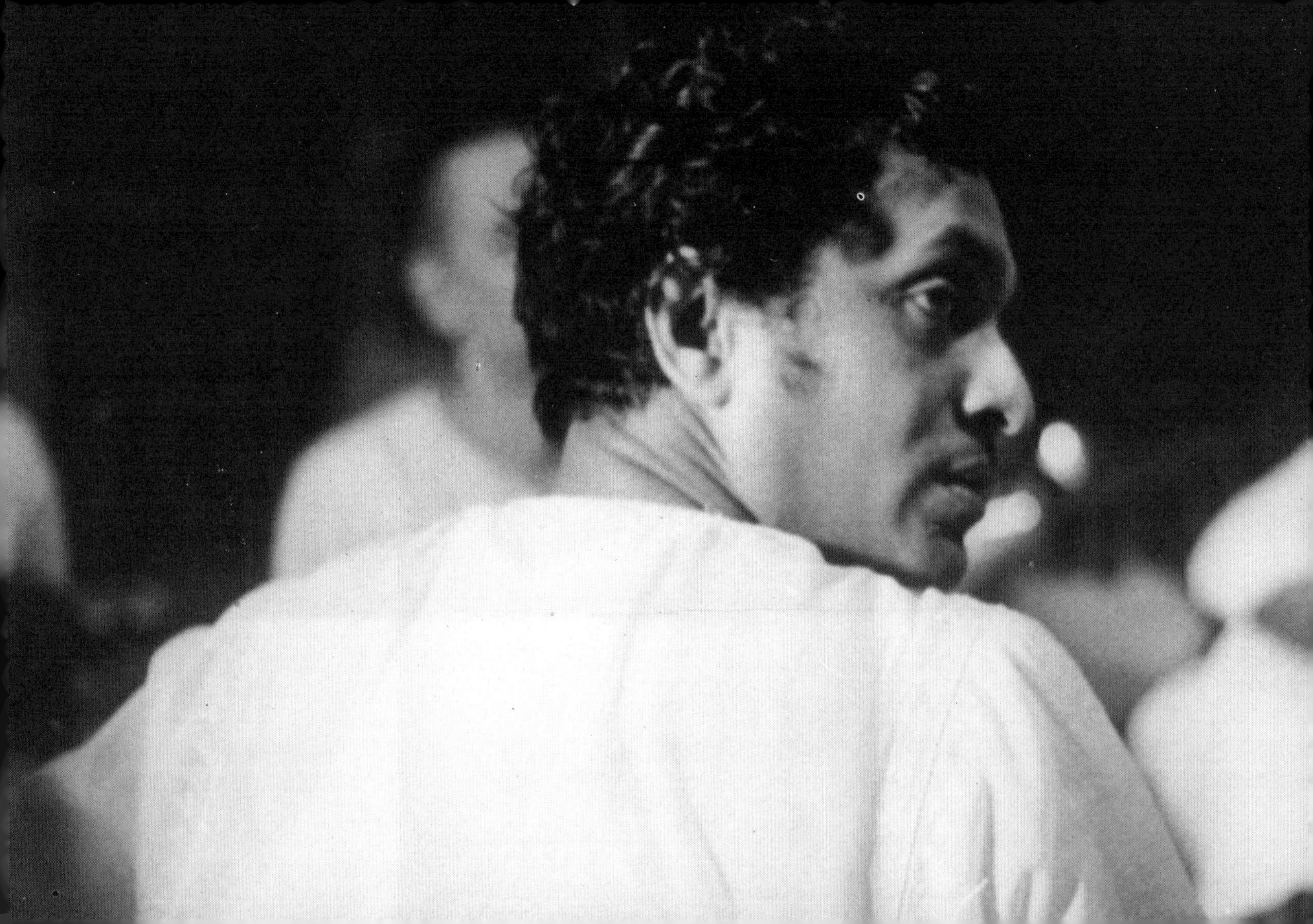

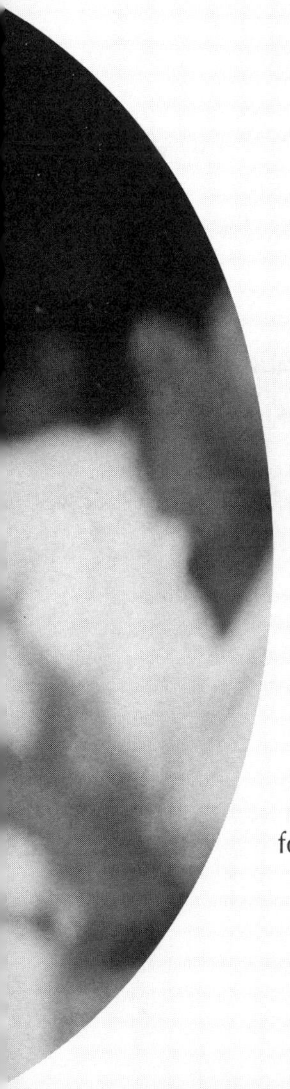

INTERVIEW WITH RAVI SHANKAR

COURTESY: *MONTAGE*, SPECIAL NO. 5-6 ON SATYAJIT RAY, JULY 1966

Satyajit Ray has been a family friend of yours since your childhood days. Can you tell us of the time when you first came to be associated with his films?

Ravi Shankar: When Satyajit Ray approached me to compose music for his film *Pather Panchali*, I agreed because we had been good friends for many years. Then when I saw the rushes of *Pather Panchali*, I was so moved emotionally. It touched a responsive chord in me, and I composed and had the music ready in exactly four-and-a-half hours. Then followed *Aparajito, Paras Pathar* and *Apur Sansar*. But for me the most moving experience was *Pather Panchali*. The rushes told me that it was a great

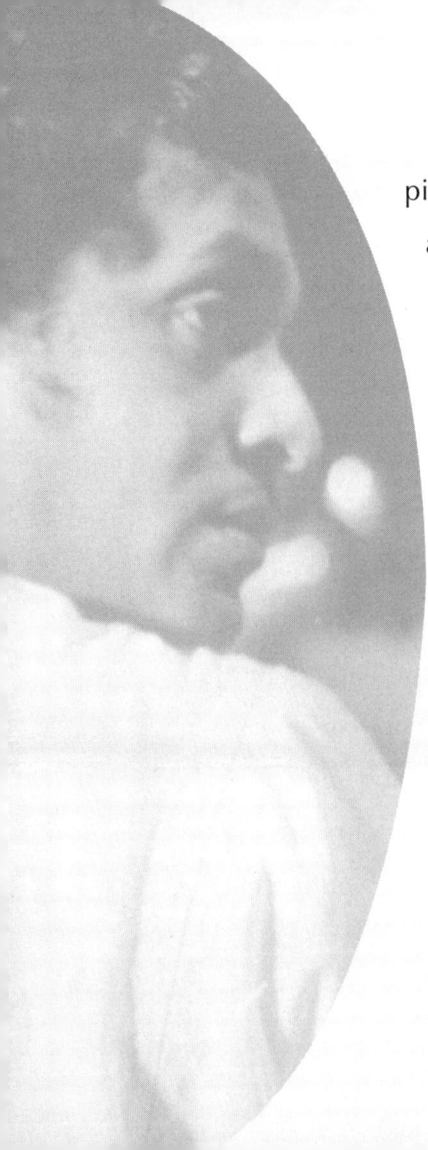

picture. There is a spontaneity about it which none of his other films have quite achieved. Every element of the film has merged so perfectly to form a cohesive whole.

What do you think of Ray as a music director?

Ravi Shankar: He is competent. He knows what he wants. He has experience in Western music, especially the piano.

Do you think a good director can function as a good music director also?

Ravi Shankar: The only person who has been good in both has been, to my knowledge, Charles Chaplin. His music in *Limelight* was superb. And yes the person one could also mention is Noel Coward.

What do you think of music directors as they function in India?

Ravi Shankar: It is difficult to say. It differs from music director to music director. Even the sound of the motor horn, chirping of birds, the lizard, and sometimes utter silence is more eloquent than any instrument, orchestra or sound. Today, film music is written in the name of classical music. Classical music is exploited to provide a veneer for popular tastes. For instance, Bade Ghulam Ali Khan's voice was used for Tansen's role in *Mughal-e-Azam*, and it is wrong. His style of singing is not that of Tansen's. There are many instances like this.

Which of Ray's own music for films have you liked?

Ravi Shankar: I like the music for the short film called *Two*.

Which of Ray's films do you like?

Ravi Shankar: I like *Kanchenjungha* and *Mahanagar*. I still think *Pather Panchali* is his best. I have a great respect for Satyajit Ray and consider him a master in the art of film direction. His films have grown from strength to strength.

Could you tell us what persuaded you to try adapting Indian classical music to background music for films?

Ravi Shankar: Well, my knowledge of classical music. In my opinion, it gives the essential background necessary for creating or adapting any kind of music.

One hears the criticism sometimes that Indian classical music cannot convey a gamut of emotions and is therefore not suitable as background music. For instance, Indian music cannot easily convey the feelings of danger, excitement, youth. This

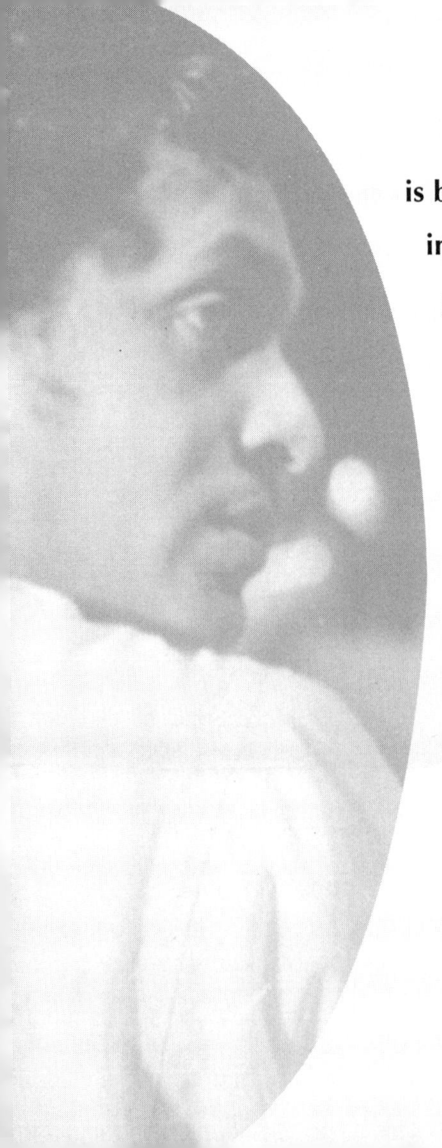

is because Indian music is inspired by religion and a philosophical concept of life. Do you agree with this view?

Ravi Shankar: It depends largely on the subject. A mixture of classical and folk music, or each by itself, can be used. It is wrong to say that Indian classical music cannot convey emotions.

You have said that you like Mr Ray's music for his short film called *Two*. Can you tell us what it is you like and what makes it memorable?

Ravi Shankar: I like the music of *Two* for its simplicity and unpretentiousness.

In what manner do you compose music for the screen? Is it possible to outline the manner in which you proceed to create the music for a film?

Ravi Shankar: It again depends on the subject. Depends on the response to the visual image.

Are you working on any film music at present?

Ravi Shankar: Yes, I am composing music for a film, *Chappaqua*, being produced in Paris by Conrad Rooks. He is an American. The story is about the quest of a man who is a lost soul. It is very interesting. Most of the work is over and I will complete the rest during my trip this summer.

You have composed music for many films. Can you tell us where you feel particularly pleased with what you have achieved?

Ravi Shankar: Mostly I have composed pieces for Ray. I like the music in *Megh* by Utpal Dutta. Its music conveys a kind of madness and discordance.

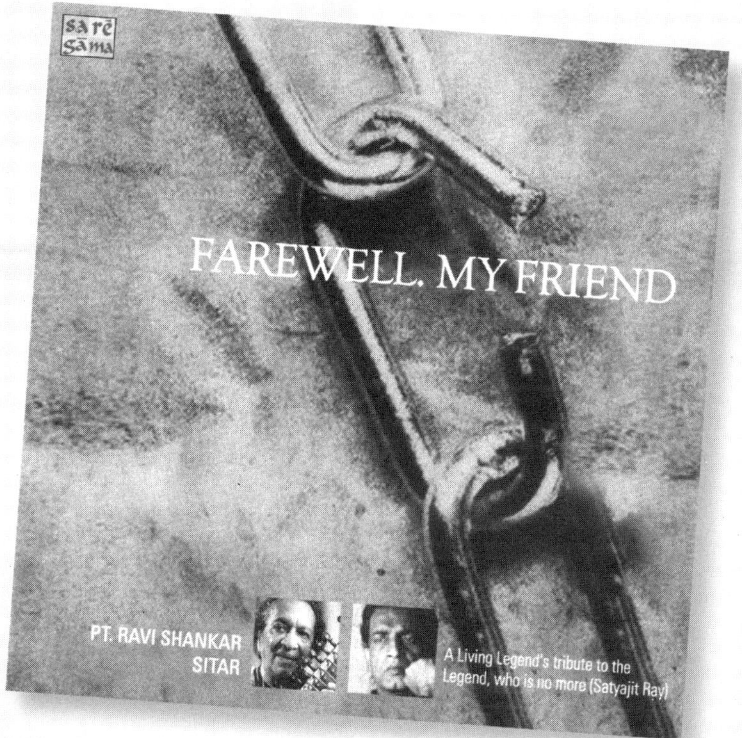

Cover of the album Ravi Shankar composed as a tribute to Satyajit Ray

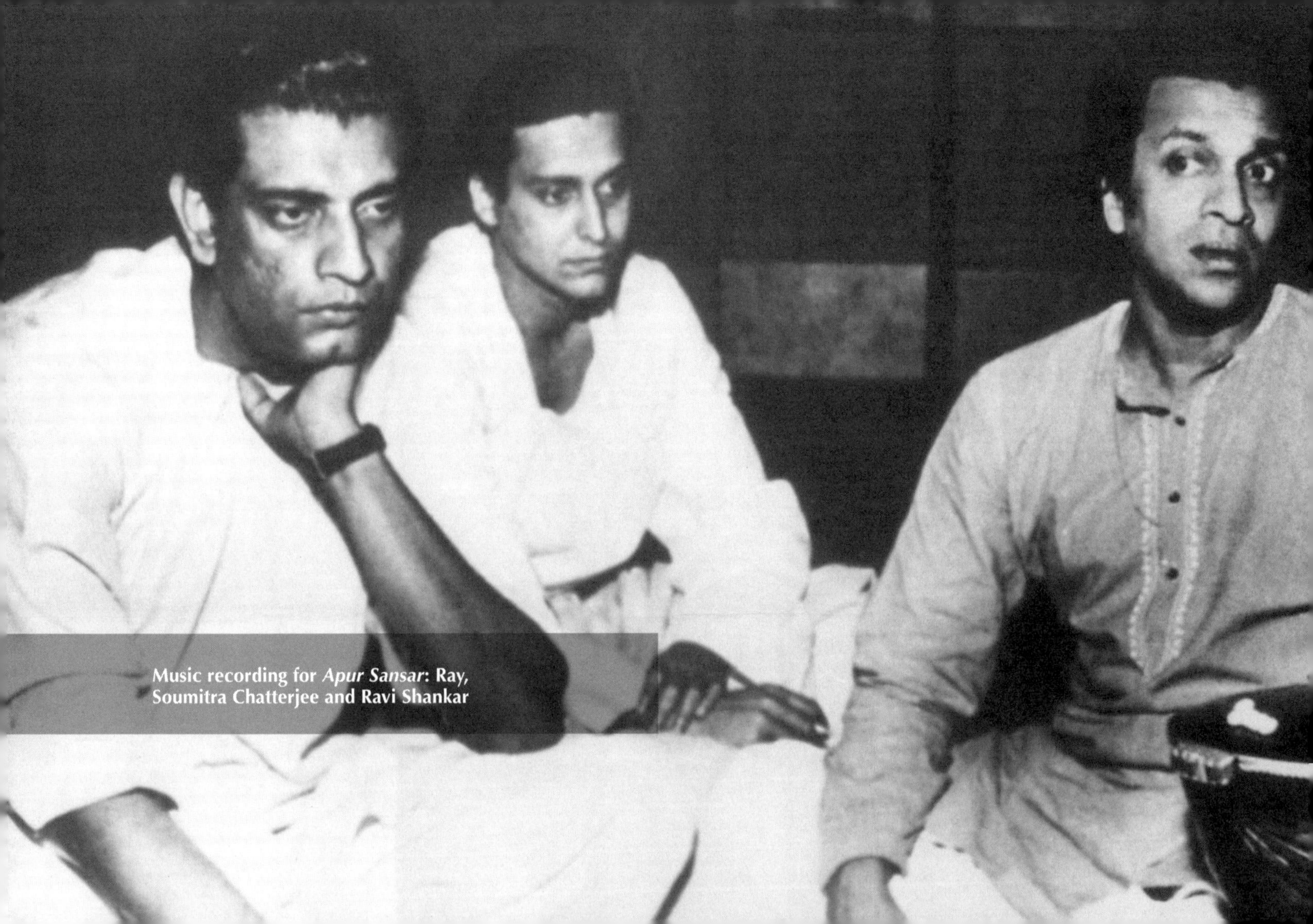

Music recording for *Apur Sansar*: Ray, Soumitra Chatterjee and Ravi Shankar

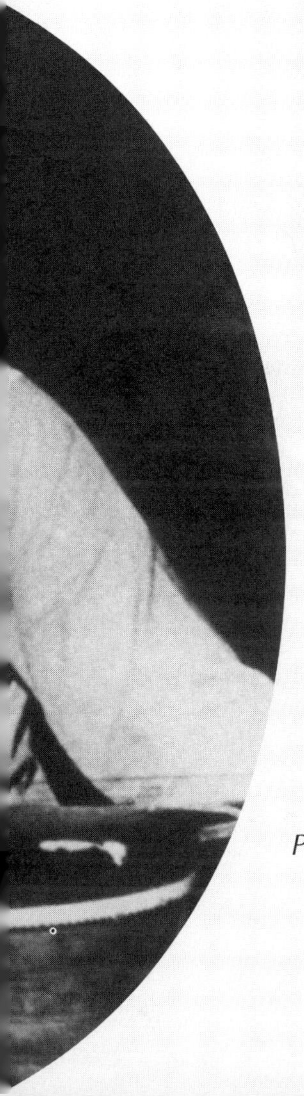

WORKING WITH SATYAJIT RAY

Ravi Shankar

EXTRACTS FROM ATANU CHAKRABARTY'S INTERVIEW WITH RAVI SHANKAR, PUBLISHED IN *MOOKHOMOOKHI RAVI SHANKAR*. TRANSLATED FROM BENGALI BY ARUP K. DE.

Pather Panchali was not the first film for which I composed music. I had done it for Khwaja Ahmad Abbas's *Dharti Ke Lal* and Chetan Anand's *Neecha Nagar* which preceded *Pather Panchali*. I also had the experience of doing music for orchestra and thematic ballet. When I watched the rough cut of *Pather Panchali*, I was moved beyond words. I worked for the film in an inspired state of mind. I still cherish that remarkable experience.

Pather Panchali, Bibhuti Bhushan's novel, and *Aparajito*, its sequel, had been serialized in leading

Bengali periodicals before they came out in book form. I heard my elders discuss them at home. So I developed an interest in these novels at a tender, pre-adolescent age. The bamboo groves and mud trails of the Bengal countryside came alive before my eyes as I read them. Bibhuti Bhushan played the most moving tune with his pen in these novels. I felt a reawakening of that tune in me while viewing the rushes of *Pather Panchali*.

Satyajit-babu requested me to compose music for *Pather Panchali* when we met at Jnanprakash Ghosh's house in Kolkata's Dixon Lane. I accepted the offer immediately. Arrangements were then hurriedly made for the viewing of the rushes at Bhavani cinema. The time for recording was fixed too.

The scoring of music for *Pather Panchali* was done in a day. I could finish my work in such a short time because Satyajit-babu had discussed the main theme of the film with me in clear terms.

I think I am able to catch the inner spirit of a certain incident or sight and then express it through music. So my mind moved musically as I watched the silent movie in the darkness of the theatre. Music was created spontaneously. As I was humming to myself, the piece that was to be the theme music of *Pather Panchali* came to me. As soon as it happened, I cried out, 'I've got it!' I didn't have to put in any extra effort for the job. I must acknowledge that I was fortunate to have brilliant musicians to work with during the music recording for *Pather Panchali*. They made my task much easier.

I've never created film music to fit exactly the lengths of scenes. Music is a tool through which I've tried to give free expression to the feelings a given scene has evoked in me. It springs from the inspiration I feel while I see a film, before I set it in musical form. 'Touching the heart' is important to me. Satyajit-babu must have been touched by Bibhuti Bhushan's novel. That, I am sure, was the reason why he wanted to make a film of it. I wrote the music for *Pather Panchali* because it touched my heart. But that's not all. *Pather Panchali* made history because it touched the hearts of audiences across the world. That's the stuff true art is made of! Being too strict about the length of a piece of music tends to kill its emotion and spontaneity. I did not create pieces of music to fill the exact lengths of scenes in *Pather Panchali,* nor in any of the other Ray films.

I used the tar shehnai instead of the violin or the sarangi for the scene of grief that followed Durga's death. The violin and the sarangi are less sharp than the tar shehnai. This instrument has the power to produce notes that are so poignant that they can, literally, pierce one's heart. I felt its use would move audiences to tears by helping them empathize with Durga's grieving parents. That I was right to choose the tar shehnai was borne out by the fact that the music brought tears to the eyes of people from all countries and nationalities who came to see the film, transcending geographical and linguistic barriers.

However, I had no role in reviving, in *Apur Sansar*, the music composed for the scene of grief in *Pather Panchali*. A director has always the freedom to examine music pieces after the recording is over, and he can use them as he pleases. It is not unnatural for a director to use, for the sake of art, the music composed for one of his films for another.

The music of *Apur Sansar* was heavier and more complex than that of the first part of the *Apu Trilogy*. The task of the title music is to give the viewers an idea of the kind of film they are going to see. The title music, in this film, anticipates the story of a larger world. It is the story of the twists and turns in Apu's life, his confrontation with the larger world and its realities, of losing his wife and getting back his child. All this combined to make his life quite complex. The crises he went through led him to a self-realization that was rather heavy. I had all these things in mind while composing the title music for the film.

I had no opportunity to be present at the time of editing any of the Ray films I had worked for. It was not possible because I was then in a 'hit-and-run' situation. I had a hectic schedule, travelling always from one place to another. I saw the films later and realized how admirably Satyajit-babu had used my music for the *Apu Trilogy*.

Satyajit-babu must have spotted some gaps in the music of *Pather Panchali* at the finishing stages. I was not close at hand. So he had to produce some additional musical effects to plug the gaps. Take, for example, the scene which shows a sweetmeat peddler going round the village to sell sweets. The scene demanded background music. So Satyajit-babu had his photographer Subrata Mitra play a beautiful piece on the sitar to fill in the gap.

Satyajit-babu never tried to impose his ideas of music on me. He was not a person who would overreact and cramp the style of his music director. We only discussed the themes of the films. Sometimes he told me the kind of music he would prefer for a particular scene, but that happened only on a few occasions. I worked in my own natural style.

I've always been a great admirer of Satyajit Ray. But it beats me why critics hesitate to acknowledge my contribution to the music of *Pather Panchali*. However, Satyajit Ray himself never failed to recognize my contributions, which is why he trusted me to score music for three more of his films (*Aparajito, Paras Pathar* and *Apur Sansar*). That he did so was eloquent testimony to his unstinted appreciation of my music.

There are people who were surprised to see Satyajit-babu take over the task of providing music for his own films after *Apur Sansar*. The reason is not far to seek. A director's mind is like the mind of a mother who is never fully happy to leave the work of looking after her child to someone else. She would always want to care for her child herself if she has the time, or feels equal to it. That is why Satyajit-babu worked as music director for all his films since *Teen Kanya*. But he never belittled others' accomplishments because he was an artist in the true sense of the word.

Satyajit-babu was a man of refined sensibilities. He had a profound understanding of music. I do not wish to discuss the music of his longer films right now. Let's take up *Pikoo*, a short film he made in 1980. The musical treatment he gave this film within the twenty-six minutes of its space was simply incomparable! The flute tune he used for *Pikoo* is still etched in my memory. It was so simple yet so powerful! You cannot forget it because of its simplicity. It appeals immediately to your heart because it is so powerful!

This is what the music of Satyajit Ray is like.

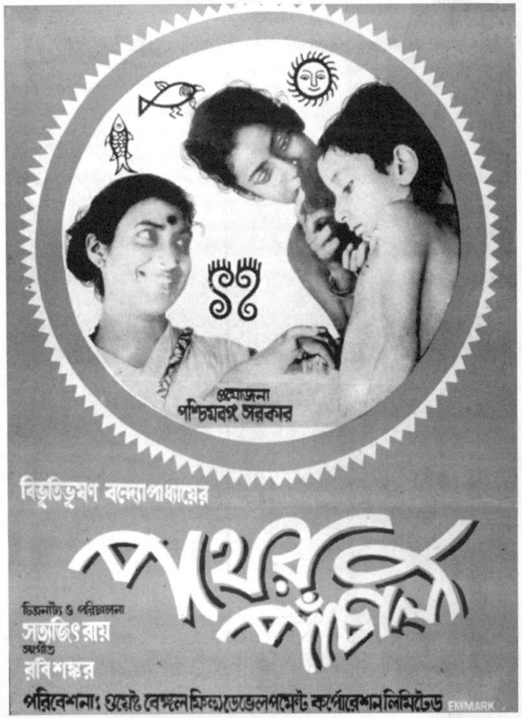

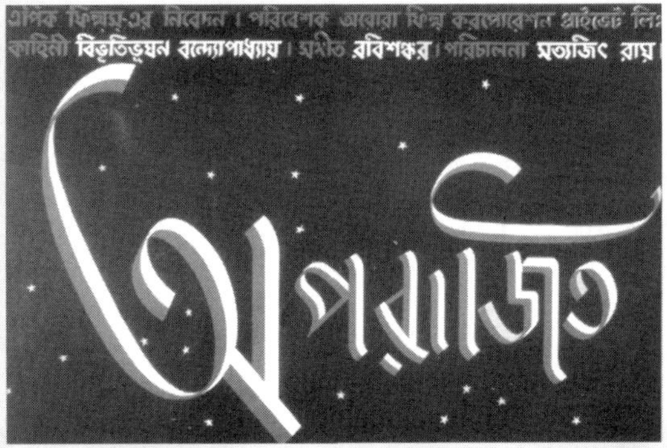

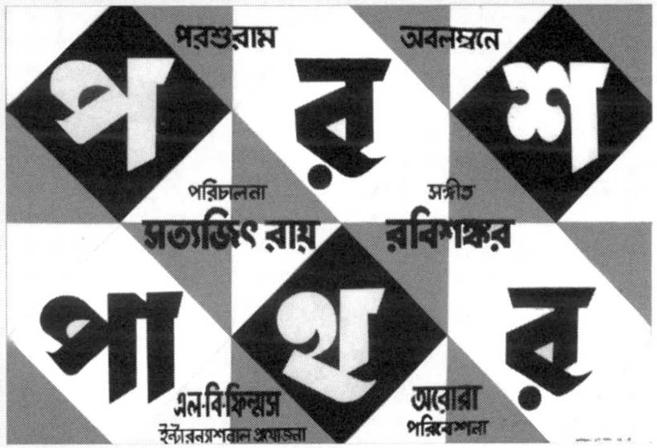

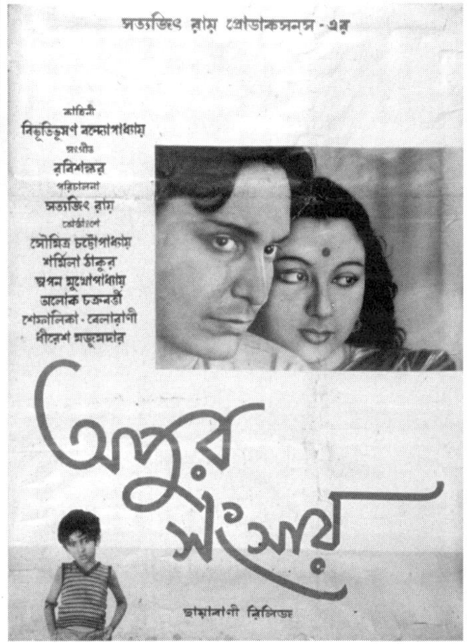

Posters for the four Satyajit Ray films—*Pather Panchali, Aparajito, Paras Pathar* and *Apur Sansar*—for which Ravi Shankar composed the music

ABOUT SATYAJIT RAY

Satyajit Ray (1921–92) was one of the greatest film-makers of his time. His first film *Pather Panchali* (1955) won an award at the Cannes Film Festival and established his reputation as a major director. Over the next forty years, he made a number of films, many of which went on to be acknowledged as all-time classics. He is the only Indian to receive the Oscar for Lifetime Achievement. He was also awarded the Bharat Ratna. His writings on cinema include *Our Films Their Films*, *Speaking of Films* and *Deep Focus: Reflections on Cinema*.

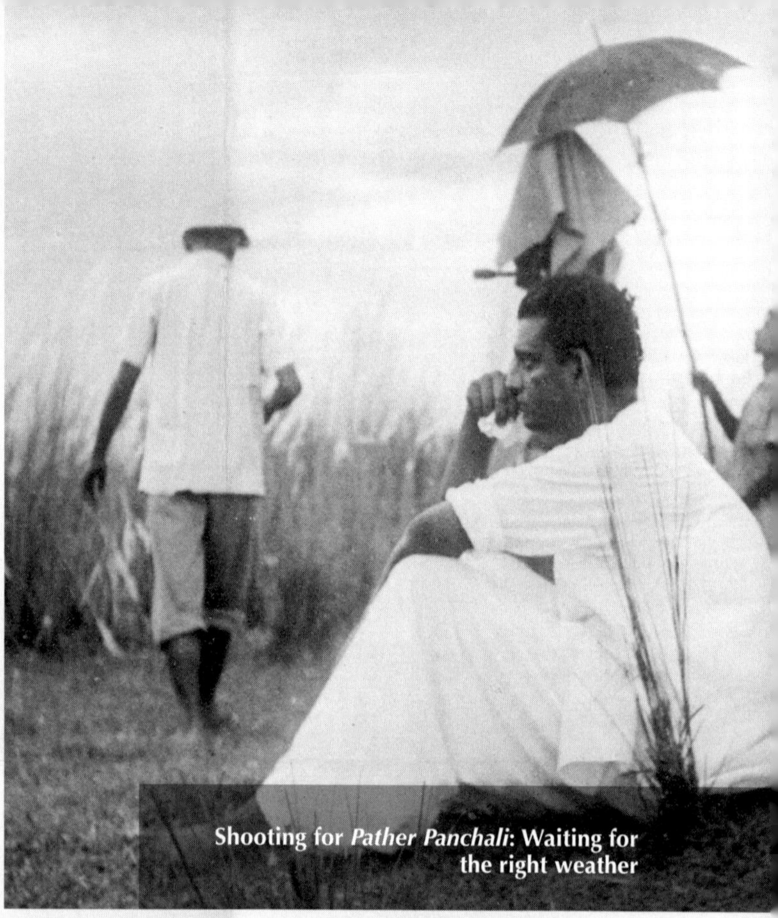

Shooting for *Pather Panchali*: Waiting for the right weather

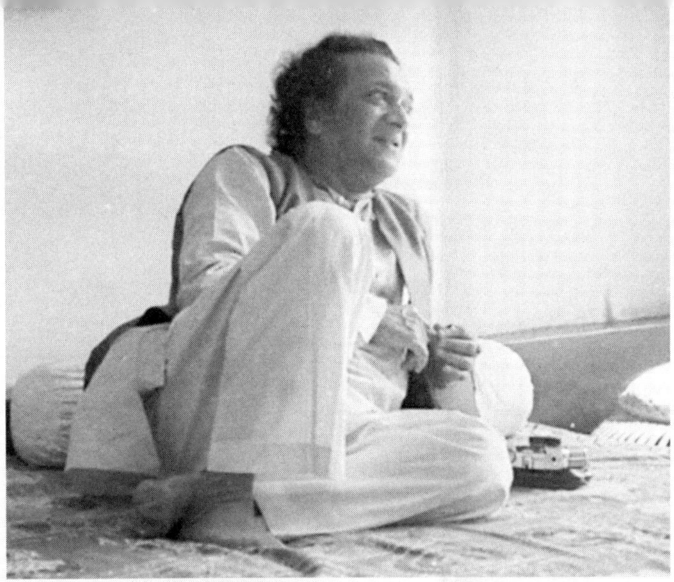

ABOUT RAVI SHANKAR

One of the greatest names in Indian classical music, Ravi Shankar (1920–2012) is credited with popularizing Indian classical music internationally. Shankar was born in Benares and spent his youth touring Europe and India with the dance group of his brother Uday Shankar. He gave up dancing in 1938 to study sitar playing under Allauddin Khan. Shankar worked as a composer, creating the music for the *Apu Trilogy* by Satyajit Ray and a number of Hindi films. In 1956, he began to tour Europe and the Americas playing Indian classical music and increased its popularity there in the 1960s through teaching, performances, and his association with violinist Yehudi Menuhin and rock artist George Harrison of the Beatles. Shankar was awarded India's highest civilian honour, the Bharat Ratna, in 1999, and received three Grammy Awards.

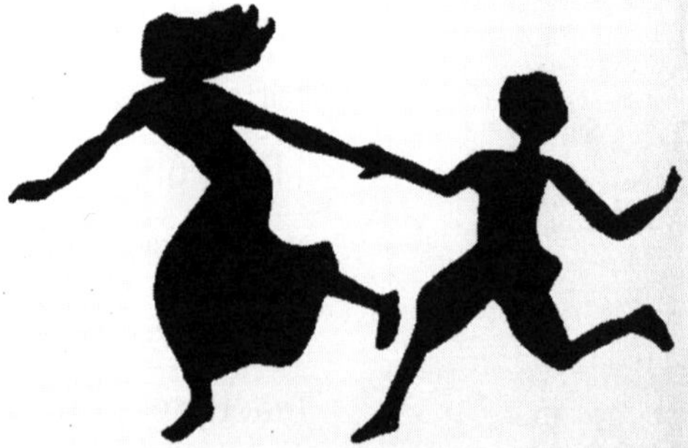

A NOTE ON THE SOCIETY FOR THE PRESERVATION OF SATYAJIT RAY ARCHIVES

PRESERVING A LEGACY

Sometime after the passing of Satyajit Ray, a number of actors and public personalities—Amitabh Bachchan and the late Ismail Merchant among them—teamed up to form what is today the Society for the Preservation of Satyajit Ray Archives (formerly the Society for the Preservation of Satyajit Ray Films). Popularly known as Satyajit Ray Society or just Ray Society, it was founded in 1994 with the object of restoring and preserving the priceless legacies left by the master director as also disseminating his work worldwide.

RAY RESTORATION

When Ray breathed his last in 1992, negatives and prints of many of his films, especially those of his early classics, were in a precarious state. David H. Shepard, a noted film preservationist in California, came to India to examine the original negatives of the Ray films. He found the negatives of eighteen of his films in 'tatters'. Restoration of Ray films was the Society's primary concern at the time. It went into a tie-up with the Los Angeles-based Academy of Motion Picture Arts and Sciences, the hallowed institution which had conferred the Oscar for Lifetime Achievement on Ray. So far, over half of the maestro's thirty-six-film oeuvre has been restored at the Academy archive. More are waiting there to mount the restoration anvil.

RAY ARCHIVES

Apart from his films, Ray left behind an astonishingly wide artistic universe comprising scripts, storyboards, posters, set, costume and book jacket designs, literary manuscripts, illustrations, music notations, advertisement artworks and so on. The Society has arguably the largest and most authentic archive on Ray in its custody. A veritable treasure trove, the Ray paper archive contains almost the entire creative output of his many-faceted genius. A large part of Ray's paper legacy has been restored under the supervision of Mike Wheeler, Senior Conservator (Paper Preservation) at the Victoria-Albert Museum, London, and is housed in his family home in Kolkata. The large personal library that Ray left as well as his personal effects is also being carefully preserved.

PUBLISHING RAY BOOKS

As part of its dissemination campaign, the Society has begun to publish books by and on Ray. It brought out *Deep Focus: Reflections on Cinema*, a collection of long-lost essays by Ray, in December 2011 in collaboration with

HarperCollins *Publishers* India. The present book is the Society's second joint venture with HarperCollins. More are in the pipeline.

RAY HERITAGE CENTRE

The Society is committed to preserving Ray's precious heritage for future generations of film lovers and scholars by giving them ready access to a one-stop repository on Ray's luminous creative output. With this in mind, the Society plans to set up, by itself or by arrangement with like-minded organizations, a Satyajit Ray Heritage Centre, complete with a library, study centre, an auditorium and exhibition and seminar halls, for promoting awareness of Satyajit Ray and his work and its dissemination among lovers of art, literature and films.

The Society appeals to donors in India and abroad to help it give Ray's splendid heritage a permanent home in Kolkata, the city where he was born and raised and where he worked all his life, the city he loved so much and celebrated in many of his films and literary works.

Website: http://www.satyajitrayworld.com/

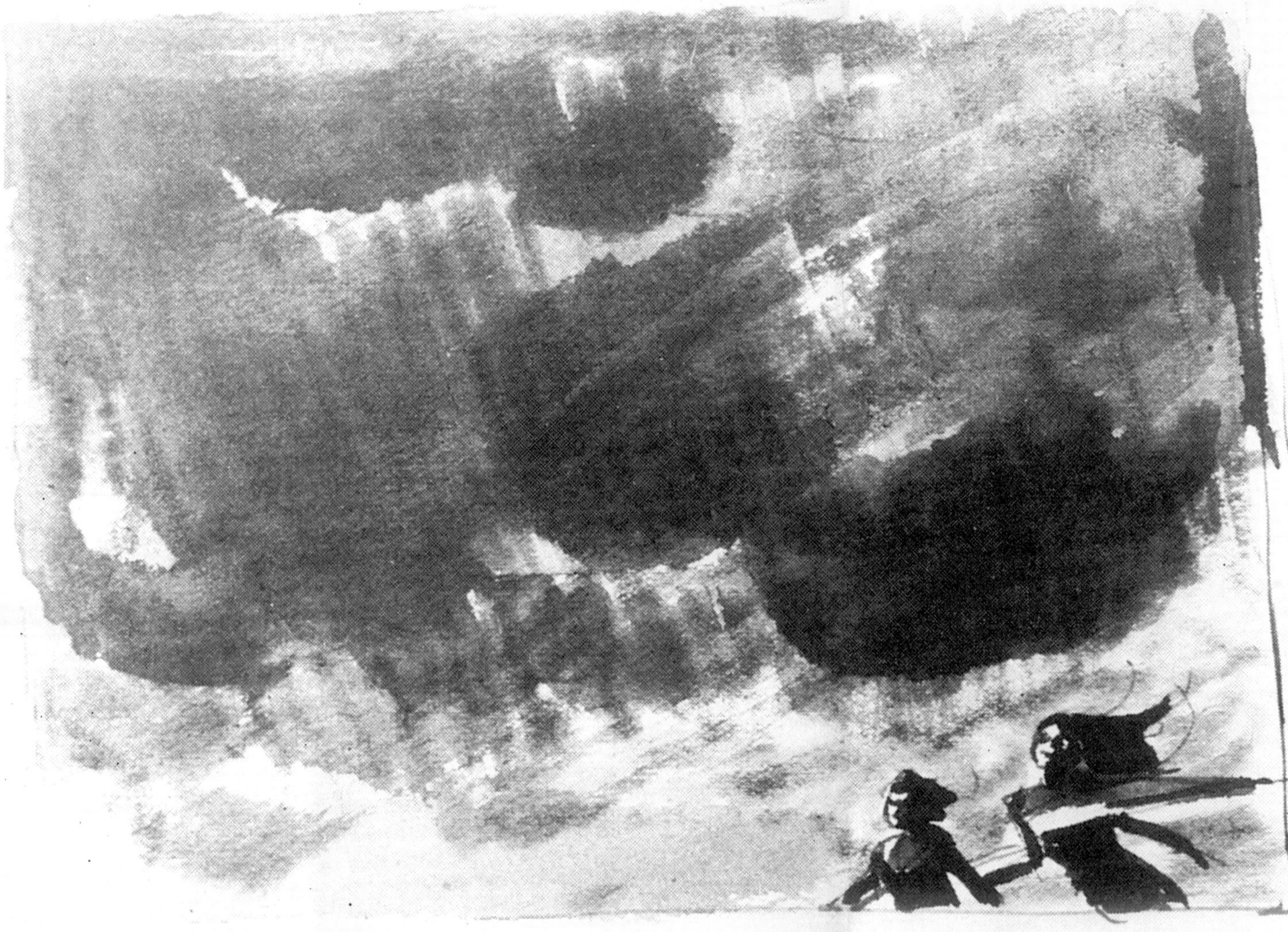

ACKNOWLEDGEMENTS

THE PUBLISHERS AND THE SOCIETY FOR THE PRESERVATION OF SATYAJIT RAY ARCHIVES WOULD LIKE TO THANK THE FOLLOWING FOR PERMISSION TO REPRODUCE TEXT FROM EXISTING BOOKS/JOURNALS:

Penguin Books India, for the extract 'Music of *Pather Panchali*' from Satyajit Ray, *My Years with Apu: A Memoir*, 1996

Montage magazine, Special No. 5-6 on Satyajit Ray, July 1966, for the interview with Ravi Shankar

Atanu Chakrabarty for extracts of the interview of Ravi Shankar published in *Mookhomookhi Ravi Shankar*, translated in this edition by Arup K. De

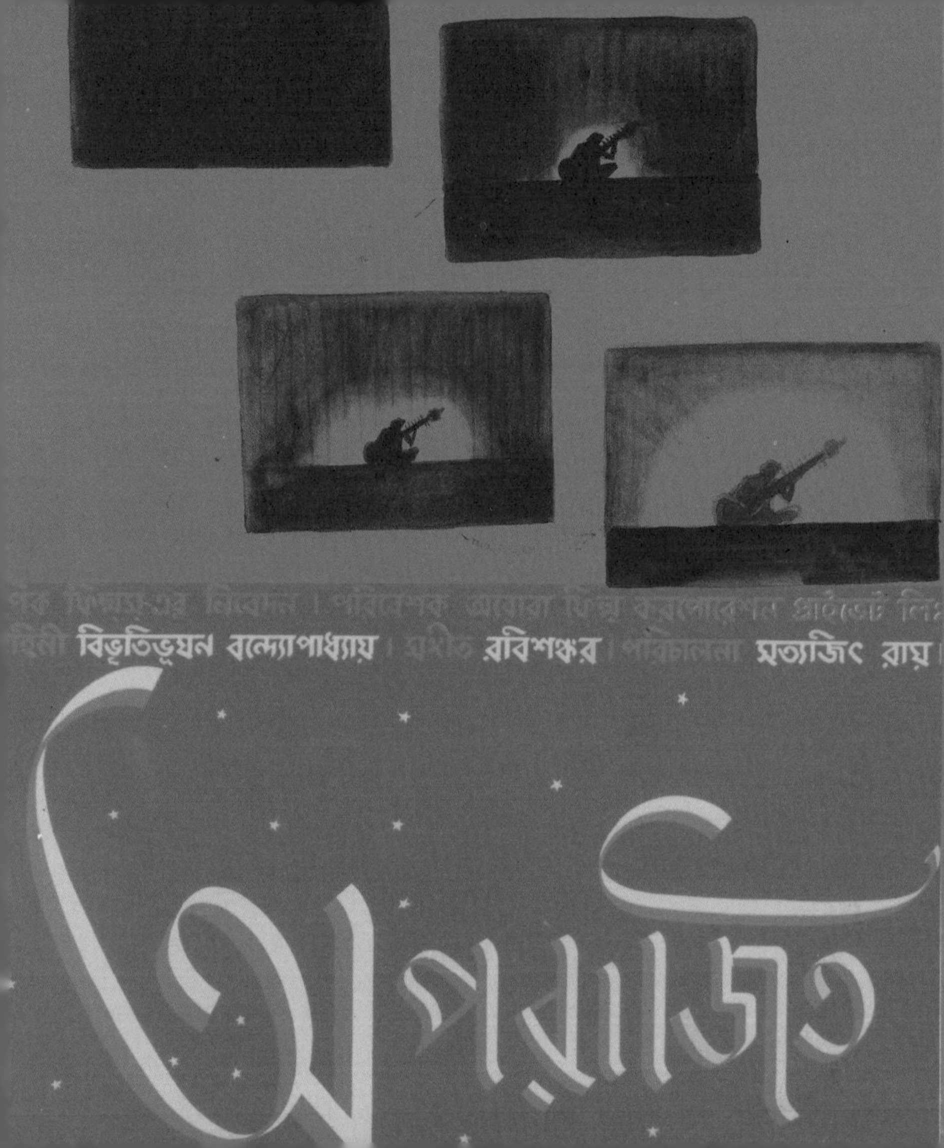
বিভূতিভূষণ বন্দ্যোপাধ্যায়
রবিশঙ্কর
সত্যজিৎ রায়
অপরাজিত

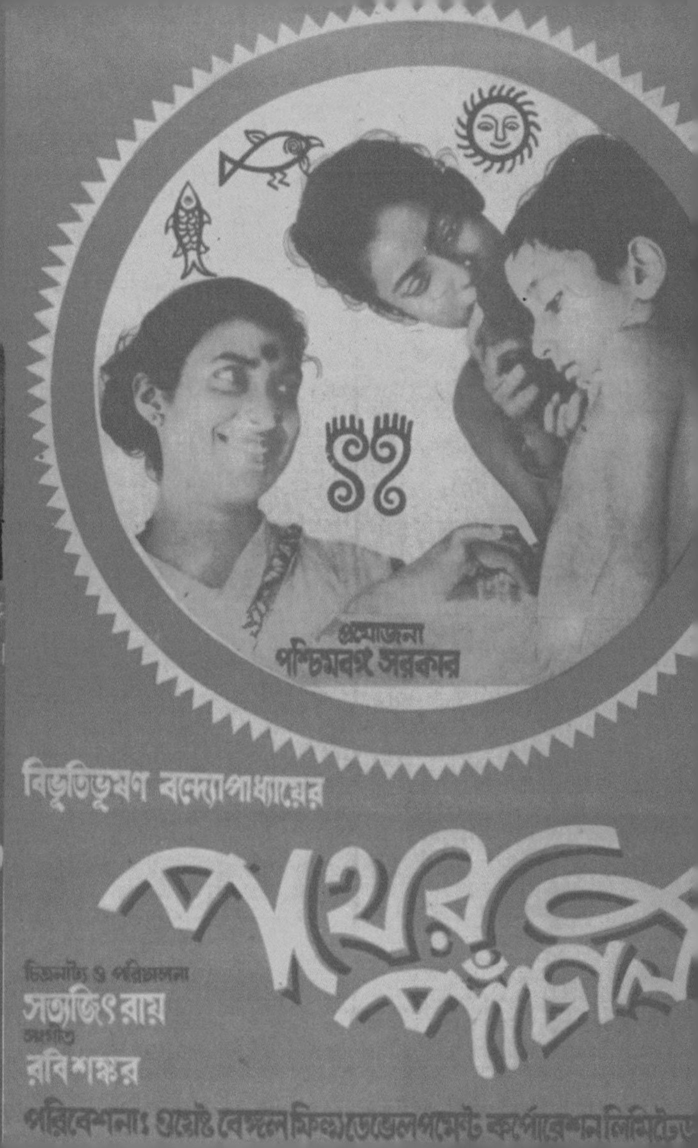
প্রযোজনা
পশ্চিমবঙ্গ সরকার
বিভূতিভূষণ বন্দ্যোপাধ্যায়ের
পথের পাঁচালী
চিত্রনাট্য ও পরিচালনা
সত্যজিৎ রায়
সংগীত
রবিশঙ্কর
পরিবেশনা: ওয়েস্ট বেঙ্গল ফিল্ম ডেভেলপমেন্ট কর্পোরেশন লিমিটেড